F. Simandl

NEW METHOD
FOR THE
DOUBLE BASS

Revised by F. Zimmermann

Edited and Annotated
by
LUCAS DREW

BOOK I

CARL FISCHER®
65 Bleecker Street, New York, NY 10012

O492
ISBN 0-8258-0152-4

Preface to the 1984 Edition. Book I.

Any method relies on the *teacher* and is a guide and a means of having an organized approach to one's study at hand. It is with the utmost respect for the legacy of Franz Simandl and the professional contributions of Frederick Zimmermann that I make the general pedagogical suggestions listed below. The music, fingerings, bowings and even the page numbers in this edition are *identical* to the *Simandl Method for Double Bass, Book I* published in 1964 and earlier Carl Fischer editions. All commentary by this editor is based upon the premise of developing a *sensitive musician* as well as a *technically proficient bassist*.

Simandl's remarks at the beginning of different sections of the book have not been changed except for possible clarification of the English translation. Comments have been added as footnotes to help up-date current thoughts and practices. In the interests of space and retaining the format of the original edition these footnotes have been placed at the end of the book (pp. 137-144). However, your teacher may also clarify Simandl's commentary in terms of his own pedagogical thoughts.

The footnotes throughout this book and the following comments offer supplementary possibilities for the use of the Simandl *Method, Book I*:

1) Use the metronome for each exercise to help proportion the bow, thereby improving tone production, bow movement and bow distribution.

2) In the early stages of study, practice a short section of an exercise and allow a measure or two rest between sections. During the silence the student has time to examine and adjust the position of his left hand as well as his bow hand and arm.

3) Possibly, study first position prior to studying half position.

4) Slurs may be introduced at any time at the discretion of the teacher.

5) When introducing a new position, a preparatory scale pattern or scale should "lead" the student to that position.

Example:

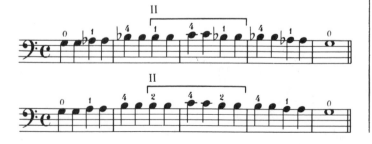

1984年版への序文
第1巻

どんな教則本であろうとも**教師**に期待するところは大きく、またそれは入門書でもあり、さらに学習者にとっては、手許に置いてその学習のための組織的アプローチの媒介となる。フランツ・シマンドルの遺産と、フレデリック・ツィンマーマンの専門的貢献とを最大限に尊重しつつ、私は以下に掲げられた一般的教育上の提言を行う。しかし、その音楽、運指、ボーイング、そしてこの版のページ数でさえも、初期のカール・フィッシャー版で、1964年に出版された**シマンドルのダブル・ベース教則本、第1巻**と同一である。この改訂者による全ての注釈は、**技術的に熟練したダブル・ベース奏者**の育成ばかりでなく、**感受性豊かな音楽家**の育成をも前提として書かれている。

本書の各章の始めの部分にあるシマンドルの注意書きについては、英訳のための文体上の変更を除き、手を加えていない。現代における広く通用した考え方や、各種練習法の助けとするために、解説が脚注として付け加えられている。紙面の関係、及び原版の形態を保存するために、これらの脚注は本書末尾に置かれている。(137頁-144頁参照)。しかしながら、各人の教師が独自の教育的思想の見解に基づき、シマンドルの解説にも変更を加える場合があり得るであろう。

本書中の脚注と後述の解説とは、シマンドル**教則本、第1巻**の利用についての補足的な可能性を提供している。

1)各練習に対して、弓の均衡がとりやすいように、メトロノームを使用すること。それによって音の出し方、弓の動かし方、弓の配分方法との向上をはかる。

2)学習の初期段階では、練習曲の短い楽節を練習し、各楽節の間には、1小節あるいは2小節の休止をとること。(休止中に学習者は、弓を持つ手や腕だけでなく、その左手の位置も調べ、調節する。)

3)ハーフ・ポジションよりも、ポジションIを先に学習することも可能であろう。

4)スラーは教師の判断で、いつ導入してもよいであろう。

5)新しいポジションを導入する場合は、予備的音階のパターン、もしくは音階によって、学習者をそのポジションに「導く」べきである。

例:

6) The teacher should point out *sequences* and *phrases* to the student throughout the book as an aid to musicianship and intonation.

7) Point out the many places to *cross-finger* in most exercises.

8) The teacher should demonstrate to the student his preferred bowing style(s) for each exercise (i.e. length of notes for detaché, martelé or slight variations of these basic "on the string" bowing styles).

9) Very few dynamics are indicated by Simandl so the teacher may wish to add them discreetly after the beginning student has developed a good concept of tone production (the full vibration of the string).

10) In general, some bowing articulations or rhythmic patterns in Parts 2, 3 and 4 of Book I may need preparatory study. The teacher is encouraged to write brief preparatory exercises using repeated pitches (or open strings) prior to introducing particular rhythms.

11) Remind the student that as the left hand moves to a higher position, in general, move the bow closer to the bridge.

12) With the teacher's guidance the student should be encouraged to increase his range vertically on the G string (or other strings) at the same time he is learning the positions horizontally (across the fingerboard).

13) Refer to *Scales, Triads, and Exercises for String Bass Beginners* (O4401) by Dmitry Shmuklovsky as a supplement to the one octave scales that are included in Simandl *Method, Book I*. All major, melodic minor, harmonic minor and chromatic scales are included in the Shmuklovksy book.

14) When possible, prepare the first finger when descending. Likewise, when ascending, prepare the fourth finger.

15) As you ascend, the distance between notes is smaller. Always be aware of the spacing of the fingers of the left hand.

16) The teacher may assign sections of Parts 2, 3 and 4 of the *Method* at any time he deems appropriate.

17) The teacher may play a simple piano accompaniment with some of the exercises. Playing with the piano helps the student develop better intonation.

This edition preserves the original and at the same time suggests other possibilities. It is hoped that the general considerations in the preface and the commentary throughout the book will aid in the continued use of Simandl's *Method*.

Lucas Drew

6）教師は、**反復進行**と**各種フレーズ**とについて、本書全体を通じて演奏法と強弱法の助言として、学習者に指摘すべきである。

7）大部分の練習曲について、**指の交差**を行うべき多くの箇所を指摘すること。

8）教師は各練習曲ごとに自分で好ましいと思う１つ、ないし複数のボーイングを学習者に実演してみせるべきである。（すなわち、デタッシェ、マルトゥレの音の長さ、あるいは、これらの基本的な「弦上の」弓使いの微妙な変化などについて。）

9）シマンドルは、強弱法についてはほとんど示していないので、教師は初心者が音を出すコツをつかんでくると、強弱法を組み入れたいと思うであろう。

10）一般的に、第１巻の第Ⅱ、Ⅲ、Ⅳ部のいくつかのボーイング・アーティキュレーション、または各種のリズム型は、予備学習を要するであろう。教師は個々のリズムを導入する前に、各種同音の繰り返し（または、各開放弦）による短い練習曲を書くようにすると良い。

11）左手が、より高いポジションに移る時は、一般的に弓を駒に近づけるよう学習者に注意すること。

12）学習者は教師の指導によって、Ｇ線（あるいは他の弦）上で、垂直方向に各自の演奏範囲を拡げて行くと同時に、（指板と交差して）各ポジションを、水平方向にも学習している。

13）シマンドルの**教則本、第１巻**に含まれているオクターヴの音階の補足として、ドミトリ・シュムクロフスキーの**ストリング・ベース初心者のための音階、３和音と練習曲**（出版番号04401）を参照すること。そこには、全ての長音階、旋律的短音階、和声的短音階、そして半音階が含まれている。

14）可能な時は、下降型では第１指を準備する。同様に、上昇の時には第４指を準備する。

15）音階が上に行くと、音と音の間隔がより小さくなる。常に左手の指のスペースに注意をはらうこと。

16）教師は、この教則本の第Ⅱ、Ⅲ、Ⅳ部を適当と思う時はいつでも学習者にあてがって良い。

17）教師は、練習曲のいくつかについて、簡単なピアノ伴奏を施すと良い。学習者にとってピアノとの共演は、より良い強弱法の上達の助けとなる。

この版は原版を保持しつつ、同時に他の可能性についても提言したものである。序文中の一般的考察と、全体を通じての解説が、シマンドルの**教則本**の継続的使用の助けとならんことを願って止まない。

ルーカス・ドゥルー

About Frederick Zimmermann

Frederick Zimmermann was born and educated in New York City. He studied Double Bass with Herman Reinshagen whom he succeeded on the faculty of the Juilliard School in 1935. Reinshagen had studied with Ludwig Manoly, a pupil of Simandl.

Zimmermann was a member of the New York Philharmonic from 1930-1966. His numerous transcriptions and editions are staples in the literature for the Double Bass. He died at the age of 61 on August 3, 1967, in Ohlstadt, Germany.

About Lucas Drew

Since 1959 Lucas Drew has been Professor of Double Bass at the University of Miami. During this period he has also been Principal Bass of the Miami Philharmonic, the Miami Opera, and the Miami Chamber Symphony. During the summer he is active as a clinician and recitalist throughout the United States and Europe.

Dr. Drew has edited many publications for Double Bass. He was editor of publications for the International Society of Bassists for eight years and is the first double bassist to hold the office of President of the American String Teachers Association (1982-1984).

フレデリック・ツィンマーマンについて

フレデリック・ツィンマーマンはニュー・ヨーク市に生まれ、同地で教育を受けた。彼はダブル・ベースをハーマン・ラインスハーゲンに師事し、1935年にはジュリアード音楽院の後任教授の地位を得た。ラインスハーゲンは、シマンドルの弟子であるルートヴィヒ・マノリに師事した。

ツィンマーマンは、1930年から1966年までニュー・ヨーク・フィルハーモニー管弦楽団の一員であった。彼による数多くのトゥランスクリフションや著作物は、ダブル・ベースのための重要な文献である。彼は1967年8月3日、ドイツのオールシュタットにおいて61才の生涯を閉じた。

ルーカス・ドゥルーについて

1959年以降、ルーカス・ドゥルーはマイアミ大学のダブル・ベース教授の要職にある。同時に、彼はマイアミ・フィルハーモニック管弦楽団、マイアミ・オペラ劇場管弦楽団、マイアミ室内管弦楽団等の主要ベース奏者をも勤めている。夏期における彼は、全米及びヨーロッパ各地において講師として、またリサイタルをするなどして活躍している。

ドゥルー博士はダブル・ベースのための数多くの出版物を監修している。彼は8年間、国際ベース奏者協会の編集委員を勤め、1982年から1984年の間はベース奏者としては初めての米国弦楽指導者連盟の会長の要職にある。

Franz Simandl (signature)

Biography

Franz Simandl was born August 1, 1840 in Blatna, Bohemia. He was a pupil of Josef Hrabe (1816-1870) at the Prague Conservatory from 1855-1861. As a performer he was the leading bassist of the Vienna Court Orchestra for many years.

Simandl was Professor of Double Bass at the Vienna Conservatory of Music from 1869 until 1910. His comprehensive method "summarized" 19th century double bass technique and included many original compositions and transcriptions for double bass and piano. Simandl died in Vienna on December 13, 1912.

伝　記

フランツ・シマンドルは1840年8月1日、ボヘミヤのブラトゥナで生まれた。彼は1855年から1861年まで、プラハ音楽院でヨゼフ・フラベ (1816－1870) の生徒であった。演奏家としての彼は、長年ヴィーン王室管弦楽団の指導的ベース奏者であった。

シマンドルは、1869年から1910年までヴィーン音楽院のダブル・ベースの教授を勤めた。彼の内容豊かな教則本は、19世紀のダブル・ベース技法を「要約」しており、しかもダブル・ベースとピアノのための数多くのオリジナル作品や、トランスクリプションを含んでいる。シマンドルは1912年12月13日、ヴィーンにて没した。

Fingering Chart*

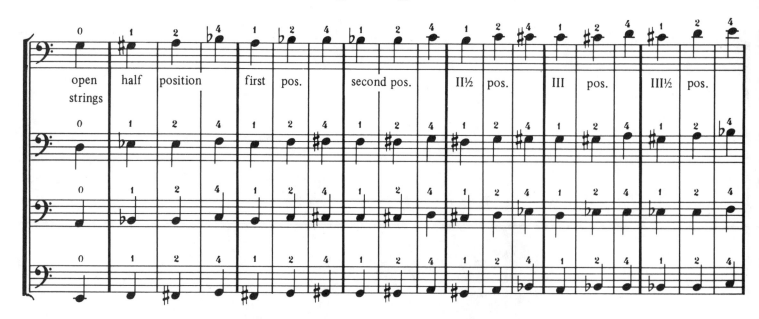

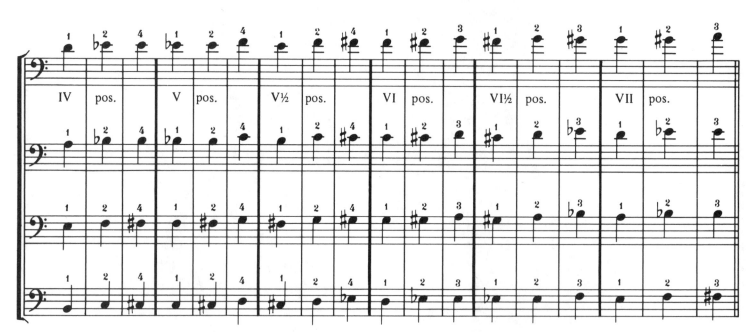

TUNING BY HARMONICS IN THIRD POSITION

1. Play an A major scale (one octave) using the second and fourth fingers respectively for G sharp and A on the D string in the third position.

Example

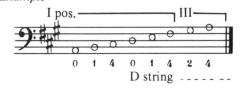

2. Touch the A (third position-D string) lightly with only the fourth finger. (measure 1)

3. This note sounds A (one octave higher than the pressed A). Adjust the D string accordingly. Turn the tuning peg clockwise to make the string higher in pitch, counterclockwise to make it lower.

4. Keeping a good left-hand position, touch lightly the D (third position) on the A string with the first finger. This also sounds A. (measure 2)

5. Match the two A's.

6. Now touch the A string lightly with the fourth finger and match it with the first finger on the E string. (measure 3)

7. Touch the D string lightly with the first finger and match it with the fourth finger on the G string. (measure 4)

8. Use a full bow (down bow on one note, up bow on the other) when tuning.

9. Always play first the harmonic or note that is on the string in tune.

* From *Scales, Triads, & Exercises for String Bass Beginners* by Dmitry Shmuklovsky Drew, Carl Fischer (O4401)

O492

運 指 表*)

ポジションIIIでのハーモニックスによる調弦方法

1) ポジションIIIでは、イ長調音階（1オクターヴ）をD線上で嬰ト音及びイ音の各々に、第2及び第4指を用いて演奏すること。
例 ポジションI

D線 ----------

2) イ音（ポジションIII、D線）は、第4指だけで軽く触れること。（第1行程）

3) この音符はイ音（指でおさえられたイ音よりオクターヴ高い）が鳴る。それによってD線を調整すること。弦のピッチを高くするには、糸巻を右回しに、低めるときは左回しにすること。

4) 正しい左手の位置を保ちながら、第1指でA線上のニ音（ポジションIII）を軽く触れる。これもまたイ音が鳴る。（第2行程）

5) 2つのイ音のピッチを合わせる。

6) 第4指で軽くA線に触れ、E線上の第1指と釣り合わせる。（第3行程）

7) 第1指で軽くD線に触れ、G線上の第4指と釣り合わせる。（第4行程）

8) 調弦の時は、弓を一杯に用いること（1つの音に対して下げ弓で、次の音に対して上げ弓で、といった具合に）。

9) 常に、先ずハーモニックスで、または調弦された弦上の音で演奏すること。

*) ドゥルー監修、シュムクロフスキー著・ストリング・ベース初心者のための音階、3和音と練習曲、カール・フィッシャー版（04401）より。

Preface
to the 4th enlarged
and improved German Edition

Although the methods for Double Bass which have appeared in print up to the present time have many good qualities, I have come to the conclusion that the majority are either not complete or are too complicated for general understanding to supply the student with a thorough education on this particular instrument in an easy and practical manner and in accordance with present-day requirements.

In consequence thereof, and in answer to a special request of the Vienna Conservatory of Music, I was prompted to write this present Method and have directed my special attention towards arranging the instructive material contained therein, in as progressive and explicit a manner as possible.

This Method has been published in two Books, and the contents have been arranged and distributed as follows:

Book I, designed as a thorough schooling for orchestral playing, contains **all the Positions**, **Major and Minor Scales**, **Intervals**, **Bowings**, **Grace Notes** together with necessary and appropriate exercises, all the various styles of **Writing for the Double Bass**, examples of **Recitative** and **Melodramatic Music**, as well as extracts from prominent and well-known Classic works.

Book II, offers a **Systematic Guide for Solo Playing** and I have aimed to present the **Thumbposition**, which up to this time has been treated in a somewhat primitive fashion, in a reformed system, in order to broaden and facilitate the domain of **Solo playing**. Furthermore a complete course of all the **Harmonics** is presented to the pupil, and numerous **Technical Exercises** and **Studies** of every grade and form, preparing him thoroughly for **Solo playing**.

In order to offer the opportunity for self-tuition to all those who are not in a position to procure the aid of an accomplished teacher, I have supplied both Books with plain and easily understood explanatory remarks, with the hope that they will add greatly to the practical value of the work.

In conclusion I will add that this Method has been introduced at the Vienna Conservatory of Music and has been received very cordially by the general public. I have achieved the quickest and most satisfactory results in a relatively short time through its use.

Franz Simandl

序　文

補筆改訂ドイツ版 第4版のために

今日出版されているダブル・ベースのための教則本は内容的に良いものが多いにもかかわらず、その多くは完全さを欠いていたり、もしくは一般的理解のためにはあまりにも複雑すぎるので、学習者に易しく実際的な方法で、しかも今日の要求に応えてこの楽器の完全な教育を施すことはできない、という結論に私は達した。

そのような理由と、ヴィーン音楽院からの特別な依頼に応えて、私はさっそくこの教則本を書き、しかもそこには段階的かつ可能な限り明解な方法で教育的要素をとり入れるような特別の配慮をした。

この教則本は2分冊で出版され、内容は以下のようになっている：

第1巻は、オーケストラ演奏のための学習教程として組まれており、**全てのポジション、長調及び短調による音階、音程、ボーイング、装飾音**などを必要かつ適当と思われる練習曲と共に導入した。また**ダブル・ベースのために作曲された**全ての異なる様式、**レシタティーヴ及びメロドラマティック音楽**の各例、そして同様にクラシック音楽よりの顕著で有名な抜粋なども取りあげられている。

第2巻は、**独奏のための体系的指導書**であり、今日まで幾分、古くさい方法で取り扱われてきた**親指のポジション**というものを改善することにより、**独奏のための領域を広げる**と共に容易にするために、ここに紹介することをねらった。さらに学習者のために、**全てのハーモニックス**の総合的学習、そして数多くの段階別、様式別による**技術練習**ならびに**練習曲**など、**独奏にかかわる**徹底的な準備がここに紹介されている。

練達の教師の助けをかりられない独学者達に供するために、私はこの2冊の本を、その実用的価値の大いに増大することを願いつつ、平易で理解し易い解説をもって表した。

終りに、私はこの教則本がヴィーン音楽院で採用され、しかも一般にも歓迎され続けていることを付け加えておく。私は、これらを使用することで 比較的短期間内に、最も速く、最も満足すべき成果を成し遂げたのである。

フランツ・シマンドル

Parts of the Double Bass

1. Scroll   2. Pegs   3. Peg Machine   4. Saddle or nut   5. Neck
6. Fingerboard 7. Top 8. Sides 9. F-or Sound Holes 10. Bridge
11. Tail-piece   12. Tail-pin or End-pin   13. Stick of the Bow
14. Bow Screw   15. Tip or Head of Bow   16. Nut or Frog
17. Hair. The Bass Bar and Sound Post are placed inside the
instrument. The reverse side of the instrument is "the Back."

ダブル・ベースの各部分名称

1. 渦巻、2. 糸巻、3. 糸巻器、4. サドルまたは上駒、5. ネック、

6. 指板、7. 面板、8. 側板、9. エフ字孔、10. 駒、11. 尾止板、

12. テール・ピンまたはエンド・ピン、13. さお、14. スクリュー、

15. 弓先、16. 毛箱、17. 毛。

「力木」と「魂柱」が楽器内部に置かれている。

楽器の裏面は「裏板」である。

O492

PHOTOGRAPHIC CHART OF CORRECT POSITIONS FOR THE DOUBLE BASS PLAYER

写真によるダブル・ベース奏者のための正しい配置図

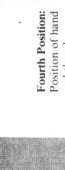
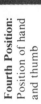

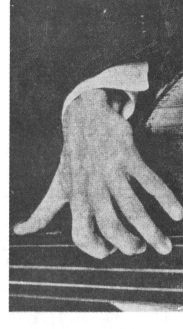

Fourth Position: Position of hand and thumb

ポジションⅣ：手と親指の位置

Seventh Position: Correct setting of all fingers

ポジションⅦ：全ての指の正しい配置

Correct Position: Showing the general position of the player, his bow and instrument, while performing.

(Posed by: FREDERICK ZIMMERMANN)

正しい位置：演奏中の奏者、弓、楽器の一般的配置

（写真はF.ツィンマーマン）

Holding the Bow: French, also known as the Bottesini method

弓の持ち方：
ボッテスィーニの教程として
も知られているフランス式

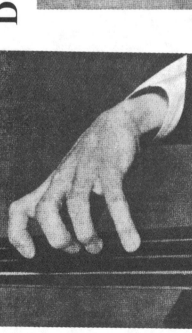
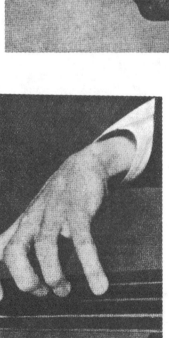

First Position: Setting of fingers

ポジションⅠ：各指の配置

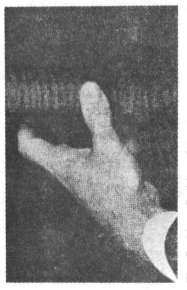

First Position: Position of thumb on neck

ポジションⅠ：ネック上の親指の位置

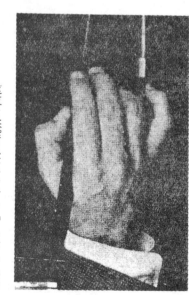

Holding the Bow (German): Correct placing of all fingers

（ドイツ式）弓の持ち方：全ての指の正しい配置

N.B. The photographs have been reproduced from the original edition.

（注）これらの写真は原版よりの複製である。

Part I.
The Position of the Player.

In taking his position next to the instrument, the player must stand in such a way that the weight of his body will be born principally by the left foot, the right foot being advanced for the distance of a short step, and in an outward direction. The body must be held as quietly as possible, and in a perfectly up-right manner. The instrument is placed in front to the left, in such a way that it will incline somewhat, but very slightly, in a backward direction towards the player, and allowing the back right edge of the instrument to fit into the left thigh of the player. (See Illustration)..

How the Bow is to be held.

The bow is held by the right hand through means of the fore and middle finger being placed in a downward direction on the side of the stick, and the ring and little finger lightly clasping the nut.

The thumb, through which the actual pressure is brought to bear upon the whole bow, is also placed in a downward direction on the back of the bow, opposite to the fore-finger, the screw coming to lay between the latter finger and the thumb. The bow receives its only contact while being used through the pressure of the thumb, as well as through the counter-pressure of the strings and the fulcrum of the screw, between thumb and fore-finger. The nut, in order that ease and dexterity may be achieved in playing, must never be pressed into the palm of the hand. (See Illustration).

How the Bow is to be drawn.

In order to draw the bow correctly it is principally necessary, that the arm is held in a natural, unrestrained manner and without coming in contact with the body. The movements of the upper arm are very slight, the elbow executing the most and the wrist being used for the most important ones. However the shoulder-joint of the upper arm must not be allowed to remain stiff, but must be kept responsive and very flexible.

The bow is drawn horizontally and its stick turned somewhat in the direction of the finger-board. It must touch the strings in the middle, between the end of the finger-board and the bridge. However, it must be observed, that whenever the tone is to be increased, the bow should be moved nearer to the bridge, as in this way, the buzzing noise, caused by the hitting of the strings against the finger-board, will be entirely avoided.

The Tuning of the Double Bass.

The Double Bass is tuned in fourths: the highest and thinist string to: [G], the next to [D], the third to: [A]

and the lowest string to: [E]

Beethoven, Cherubini, R. Wagner and many of our modern composers have written bass parts for some of their works, which make it necessary to tune the 4th string down to low C or C sharp. In order to bring this about without extra exertions, Mr. Carl Otho, a member of the Leipzig Gewandhaus Orchestra, has invented an appliance for the Double Bass, which makes it possible to produce the Contra C upon the instrument. With its aid the intentions of the composers in this special direction can be satisfactorily fulfilled without necessitating the re-tuning of the instrument by the player. He has simply added a fifth string to the Double Bass and the result has been a very successful one. Hans von Bülow made use of these 5-stringed Double Basses in his cycles of Beethoven concerts and quite a number have been introduced in our larger modern symphony orchestras.

F.S.

第Ⅰ部
奏者の位置

奏者は楽器の後に位置し、基本的にその体重を左足にかけ、右足は短い歩はばの1歩分だけ外側へ踏み出す形で立たなければならない。身体は、できるだけ静止状態にし、完全な直立姿勢をとる。楽器は左正面に置き、幾分ごくわずかに後方へ奏者側に傾斜させる。そして楽器の右はじの裏板部分は、奏者の左大腿部にあてがう。（写真参照）

弓はどのように持つか

弓は右手で持ち、人差し指と中指を、さおの下方側面に置き、薬指と小指は軽く毛箱を握る。

親指にかかる力は、弓全体に影響を及ぼす。この指も、やはり弓の根元の背側に置き、人差し指と反対側にくる。スクリューは、親指と残りの指との間にくる。弓は使用されている間、親指と人差し指の間にはさまれて弦の反発力とスクリューの支点を通じてと、親指にかかる力を通じての影響だけを受ける。毛箱については、容易に機敏な演奏を行うために、決して手のひらできつく握ってはならない。（写真参照）

弓はどのようにして動かすか

弓を正しく動かすためには、腕を自然のまま、身体と接触させずに自由な状態にしておくことが基本的に大切である。上腕部の動きは、ごくわずかであり、肘と手首の動きが最も重要である。しかし肩の関節は、こわばっていてはならず、常に大変柔軟な対応ができなければならない。

弓は水平にひかれ、さおは幾分、指板の方へ傾け、指板の端と駒の間の弦の中央部分に接触させなければならない。しかしながら音量を増す時は、常に弓を駒に近づけておかなければならない。このようにすることにより、弦が指板に当って起きる雑音は完全に防止できるであろう。

ダブル・ベースの調弦

ダブル・ベースは4度ごとに調弦される。最高音の最も細い弦は [G] 次は [D] 第3番目は [A] そして 最低音の弦は [E] である。

ベートーヴェン、ケルビーニ、R.ヴァーグナー、そして多くの近代の作曲家たちは、彼らの作品の中で、そのベース・パートに第4線を調弦して低めなければならない「ハ音」または「嬰ハ音」を書いている。これらの音を、特別な苦労をすることなく生じさせるために、ライプツィヒ・ゲヴァントハウス管弦楽団のカール・オットー氏は、この楽器で低い「ハ音」を出すことのできる仕掛けを発明した。この発明の助けにより、作曲家たちの特別な音域への意向は、奏者による再調弦の必要性なしに、充分に満足の行く解決を見た。彼は、ただ第5弦を加えただけであるが、その結果は大成功であった。ハンス・フォン・ビュロウは、彼が催したベートーヴェン連続演奏会に、この5弦ダブル・ベースを用いて、はなはだしい回数、広く我々の時代の近代的オーケストラに紹介を行ったのである。 F.S.

6

Explanation of the Signs for the Bow.

⊓ Down Bow   ∨ Up Bow
N. at the Nut or Frog ⎫
T. at the Tip or Point ⎬ of the Bow.
M. in the Middle ⎭

Exercises on the Open Strings. [1]

Place the bow upon the strings close to the nut and draw it down and up slowly and lightly as marked in the following exercises.

開放弦での練習 [1]

弓の毛箱に近い部分を弦の上に置き、下げ弓、上げ弓の順で次の各練習に記るされた記号に従って、ゆっくり、そして軽く動かす。

[1] All editorial footnotes will be found at the back of the book on pages 137-144.

[1] 全ての脚注は巻末の137頁から144頁を参照。

O492

Exercises on the G, D, A and E String in Whole, Half and Quarter notes.

G線, D線, A線及びE線上での練習
全音符, 2分音符, 4分音符による

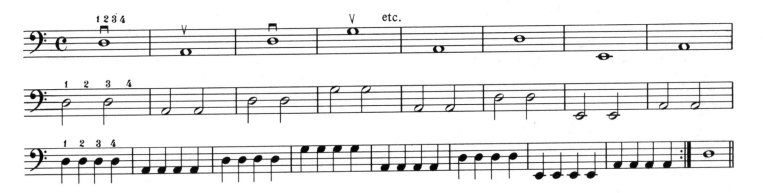

These exercises on the open strings are to be practiced until a firm and graceful command of the bow and its manipulation has been acquired; constantly observing the rules as to position of the body, together with those for the correct position and use of the bow.

これらの開放弦上での練習は、弓のしっかりとした優美な操作が習得されるまで練習されなければならない。身体の位置と弓の正しい配置、および用法は常に原則として守らなければならない。

The Positions.

The placement of the fingers of the left hand upon a higher or lower point of the finger-board is indicated as a position. As the hand may be advanced to different points of the finger-board we distinguish different positions; commencing at the nut or saddle and advancing in steps of one half-tone, these are named according to the higher or lower position of the interval. For orchestral playing more than twelve positions are seldom employed these being divided into the "usual" or "half," seven "whole" positions and "four" "intermediate" positions. In addition to these there is the "Thumb-position," which is rarely employed in the orchestra but which is frequently used in solo playing. Detailed explanation of this last named position, as well as of the harmonics occuring in the various positions, will be found in Book II. **2**

各ポジション

指板上の上方、または下方に置かれる左手の指の配置は、ポジションとして表示される。指板上の異なる位置へ手が進んだ場合においては、違ったポジション分類をする。上駒の部分から始めて、半音ずつ段階的に前進させる。これらは、その音程の位置の高低に従って名付けられる。オーケストラ演奏においては、ごくまれに12以上のポジションが使用され、これらは「通常」または「ハーフ」と、7つの「全」ポジション、及び「4つ」の「中間」ポジションとに分割される。これに加えて、オーケストラではまれであるが、独奏ではしばしば用いられる「親指のポジション」がある。この最後の名称のポジションと、様々なポジションによって生ずるハーモニックスについての詳細な説明は、第2巻で行うことにする。**2**

Explanation of the signs for the Positions.

h.P. indicates the usual or "half" Position.
I. " " first Position.
II. " " second "
III. " " third "
IV. " " fourth "
V. " " fifth "
VI. " " sixth "
VII. " " seventh "

[II / III denotes that the notes are between the second and third position.

[III / IV " " " " " " " third " fourth "

[V / VI " " " " " " " fifth " sixth "

[VI / VII " " " " " " " sixth " seventh "

‾‾‾ or ········· indicates, that those notes over which the sign is placed, are to be played in one position.

ポジションの表示記号の説明

h.P. は、通常または「ハーフ」・ポジションを示す。
I. " 第1ポジションを示す。
II. " 第2 "
III. " 第3 "
IV. " 第4 "
V. " 第5 "
VI. " 第6 "
VII. " 第7 "

[II / III は、第2及び第3ポジションの中間の音を示す。

[III / IV " 第3 " 第4 "

[V / VI " 第5 " 第6 "

[VI / VII " 第6 " 第7 "

‾‾‾ または ········· の記号でかぶされた音符は、同一ポジションで演奏される。

The Position of the Left Hand.

The ball of the thumb is placed against the neck of the instrument in such a position, that beginning with the "half" position, the thumb will come to stand between the fore and middle finger up to the V Position. The strings must be pressed down firmly with the tips of the fingers in order to produce a clear and voluminous tone. Also, the fingers must be well separated and stretched apart, particularly in the "half" and "first" position. While the forefinger is placed in an upward and the small finger in a downward direction, the two middle fingers retain their natural position in pressing down the strings. The holding of the arm must be free, unrestrained, and entirely in accordance with whatever movements the hand is called upon to execute. The above-described position of the hand must also be retained while changing in the different positions. Beginning with the V Position, the position of the hand is gradually changed, and a detailed explanation therefore will follow.

Explanatory Remarks on Fingering.

As the finger-board of the Double Bass is so much larger than that attached to any of the other Stringed Instruments, it is plain, that in its division (mensur) the intervals will be found at a much greater distance from each other, and that in consequence the treatment, as far as the fingering is concerned, must be a radically different one.

In this way the first, second and fourth fingers are at the command of the player up to the VI Position, an interval of one-half tone lying between the first and second and second and fourth fingers.

The third finger serves as support to the fourth and only comes into actual use in the VI Position, where it is used in place of the fourth finger, the latter not being long enough.* In pressing down a string with the first finger, the remaining unemployed three fingers must be slightly raised. While playing with the second, the first finger must remain upon the string and assist the second in pressing it against the finger-board. In a like manner the third finger must be supported by the first and second and the fourth by the first, second and third. **3**

Explanation of the Signs for the Fingers.

0 Open String.
1 First Finger.
2 Second "
3 Third "
4 Fourth "

The "Usual" or "Half" Position.

If the first finger is placed upon the finger-board one half-tone higher than the open string, the hand will be in the "Usual or Half Position." Half-position also contains the following other half-tones:

左手の位置

「ハーフ」ポジションで開始するに当り、親指の腹は楽器のネック部分に置かれ、ポジションVに至るまで、親指は、人差し指と中指の中間に位置する。弦は、はっきりとした、しかも豊かな音を得るために指先でしっかりとおさえられなければならない。とりわけ「ハーフ」と「第1」のポジションにおいては、各々の指は完全に独立して、よく広がるようにしておかなければならない。人差し指が上方に、そして小指が下方に置かれた状態では、中指と薬指は、その自然な位置において弦をおさえる。楽器をささえる左腕は、演奏上の必要に応じられるように、拘束されることなく自由な状態になければならない。以上に述べた手の配置は、他のポジションにおいても同様に守らなければならない。ポジションVで開始するに当っては、手の配置は段階的に変更されて行くが、それらについての詳細な説明は、後述する。

運指に関する注意説明

ダブル・ベースの指板は、他のどんな弦楽器に付けられたそれにくらべても、大変に大きなものであり、平たく、各指の間隔幅は他の各楽器より大変に広く、その取り扱いは、運指に関する限り全く異った存在である。

このような状況のもとで、半音々程は、第1と第2指、及び第2と第4指の間に各々生じ、ポジションVIに至るまで、これら第1、第2、第4指は、容易に奏者の要求に応じられる。

第3指は、ポジションVIの実際的使用において、次にくる充分な長さを持ち得ない第4指*の代りに、それの補助をつとめるだけである。第1指により弦をおさえる場合は、残りの3本の指は、わずかに弦からあげておかなければならない。第2指による演奏中は、第1指は弦上に留まらなければならず、第2指が指板をおさえる補助をつとめる。同様な方法で、第3指は、第1、第2指によって、第4指は第1、第2及び第3指によって補助されなければならない。**3**

指に関する表示記号の説明

0 開放弦
1 第1指
2 第2 "
3 第3 "
4 第4 "

「通常」または「ハーフ」ポジション

もし第1指が、開放弦より半音高い位置で指板上に置かれている場合、手は「通常またはハーフ・ポジション」の状態にある。ハーフ・ポジションは、次の各半音を含んでいる。

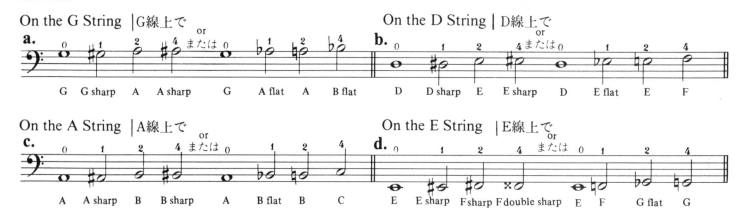

On the G String | G線上で
On the D String | D線上で
On the A String | A線上で
On the E String | E線上で

* See explanation of the VI Position, page 36.

* 36頁、ポジションVIの説明を参照。

Exercises on the Separate Strings.　　　各弦ごとの練習

Exercises for the Connection of the Four Strings.[4]　　　4 本の弦上での練習[4]

10

F Major Scale | ヘ長調音階

5.

6.

B flat Major Scale | 変ロ長調音階

7.

O492

The I. Position.

In moving one-half tone higher from the "Half" Position, the hand is placed in the "First" Position, which contains the following intervals:

ポジション I

「ハーフ」ポジションより半音高く移動する場合、手の位置は「第 1」ポジションに置かれ、次の各音程を含む。

12

Exercises in the "Half" and I. Position.　　ポジション「ハーフ」と「Ｉ」の練習

The II. Position [10]

The hand is placed in the Second Position if it is moved one-half tone higher than the First Position. It embraces the following intervals

ポジション II [10]

ポジション I より半音高く移動した場合には、手の位置は ポジション II になる。

On the G String | G線上で

a.

B flat　C flat　C　　　A sharp　B　B sharp

On the D String | D線上で

b.

F　G flat　G　　　E sharp　F sharp　F double sharp

On the A String | A線上で

c.

C　D flat　D　　　B sharp　C sharp　C double sharp

On the E String | E線上で

d.

G　A flat　A　　　F double sharp　G sharp　G double sharp

Exercises on the Separate Strings.

各弦ごとの練習

On the G String

G線上で

e.

On the D String

D線上で

f.

On the A String

A線上で

g.

On the E String

E線上で

h.

**Exercises in the II. Position
on all the Strings.**

全ての弦上での
ポジションⅡの練習

Exercises in the I. and II. Position.

ポジションⅠとⅡの練習

C Major Scale. | ハ長調音階

16

Exercises in Syncopated Notes in the II. Position.
in connection with the "Half" and I. Position.

Notes, introduced upon a light beat of a bar and connected with a heavy one, are designated as syncopated notes.

While the syncopated notes may be written in a variety of ways, their manner of playing always remains the same.

It is immaterial whether a light or heavy beat is syncopated in one note or whether the note of the light beat is slurred to the next note or an extending dot, the two syncopated parts of a bar must always be played in one bow, and the light beat of every syncopated note must be prominently accented.

Exercise, in which the light and heavy beat of a bar are syncopated in one note.

ポジション「ハーフ」と「Ⅰ」に関連する
ポジションⅡでのシンコペーションの練習

ある小節の弱拍音と、それに結びつけられた強拍音は、シンコペーションと呼ばれる。

シンコペーションは、様々な形で現われるが、その演奏方法は常に一様である。

ある音について弱拍部、または強拍部が切分されようと、弱拍音が次の音、または延長された点へタイで結ばれようと、それらは重要な事柄ではなく、ある小節のシンコペーションによる2つの音符は、常に一弓で弾かれなければならない。そして、全てのシンコペーションの頭の音符は、顕著なアクセントをもって演奏されなければならない。

1つの小節の弱拍と強拍が、**1つの音符**でシンコペーションになっている場合の練習

Exercise, in which the syncopated notes are connected with a slur.

2.

1つの**タイ**によって接合され、シンコペーションになっている場合の練習

Exercise in which the heavy beat of the bar is represented by a dot, the latter being connected with the light beat by means of a slur.

3.

1つの点により、その小節の強拍が代行され、それがタイの方法で弱拍と接合されている場合の練習

17

Exercise for the three varieties of syncopated notes.

3種類のシンコペーションのための練習

O492

18

Between the II. and III. Position
an Intermediate Position

lies one-half tone higher than the II. Position.

The following intervals are contained therein:

On the G String |G線上で   On the D String. | D線上で

C flat   C   D flat   B   B sharp.   C sharp   G flat   G   A flat   F sharp   F double sharp   G sharp

On the A String |A線上で   On the E String | E線上で

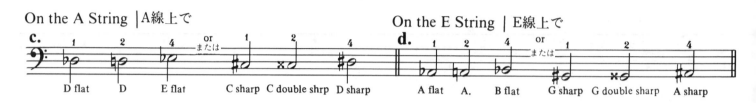

D flat   D   E flat   C sharp   C double shrp   D sharp   A flat   A.   B flat   G sharp   G double sharp   A sharp

Exercises on the Separate Strings.   各弦上での練習

On the G String / G線上で

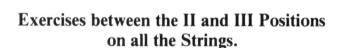

On the D String / D線上で

On the A String / A線上で

On the E String / E線上で

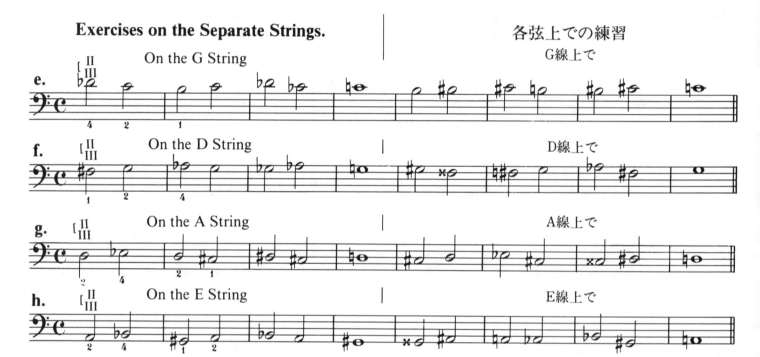

Exercises between the II and III Positions
on all the Strings.

全ての弦上での
ポジションⅡとⅢの練習

1.

2.

O492

Exercises between the II. and III. Position, in connection with the "Half" and "First" Positions.

ポジション「ハーフ」と「I」に関連した
ポジション II と III の間の練習

D flat Major Scale ｜ 変ニ長調音階

20

A flat Major Scale.　変イ長調音階

O492

The III. Position

is found one whole tone away from the second and one-half tone away from the preceding intermediate position, and contains the following intervals:

ポジションⅢ

ポジションⅢは、ポジションⅡと1音の隔りを持ち、先行する中間ポジションとは半音の隔りがあり、次の各音程を含む。

Exercises in the III. Position together with the preceding Positions.

先行ポジションを伴う
ポジションⅢの練習

D Major Scale. | ニ長調音階

A Major Scale. | イ長調音階

Intermediate Position between the III. and IV. Position.

In order to play in this position the hand must be moved one-half tone higher than the III. Position. It embraces the following intervals:

ポジションⅢとⅣの間の

中間ポジション

このポジションで演奏するためには、手の位置はポジションⅢより半音高く置かれなければならない。次の各音程を含む。

On the G String ｜G線上で

On the D String ｜D線上で

a. D flat　D　E flat　C sharp　C double sharp　D sharp

b. A flat　A　B flat　G sharp　G double sharp　A sharp

On the A String ｜A線上で

On the E String ｜E線上で

c. E flat　E　F　D sharp　D double sharp　E sharp

d. B flat　B　C　A sharp　A double sharp　B sharp

Exercises on the Separate Strings.

各弦ごとの練習

e. On the G String　G線上で

f. On the D String　D線上で

g. On the A String　A線上で

h. On the E String　E線上で

Exercises between the III. and IV. Positions on all the Strings.

全ての弦上での

ポジションⅢとⅣの間の練習

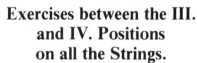

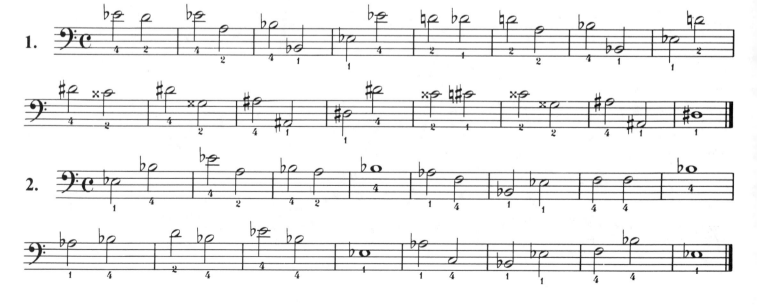

1.

2.

Exercises between the III. and IV. Positions together with the preceding Positions.

先行ポジションを伴う
ポジションIIIとIVの間の練習

E flat Major Scale. | 変ホ長調音階

B flat Major Scale. │変ロ長調音階

The IV. Position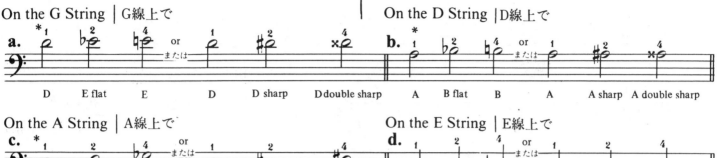

is separated from the Third by one whole, and from the preceding Intermediate Position by one-half tone, and contains the following intervals:

ポジション Ⅳ

ポジションⅣは、ポジションⅢと1音の隔りを持ち、先行する中間ポジションとは半音の隔りがあり、次の各音程を含む。

On the G String｜G線上で　　　　　　　On the D String｜D線上で

On the A String｜A線上で　　　　　　　On the E String｜E線上で

Exercises on the Separate Strings.

各弦ごとの練習

Exercises in the IV. Position on all the Strings.

全ての弦上での ポジションⅣの練習

* = 27

Exercises in the IV. Position together with the preceding Positions.

E Major Scale | ホ長調音階

B Major Scale | ロ長調音階

or
または

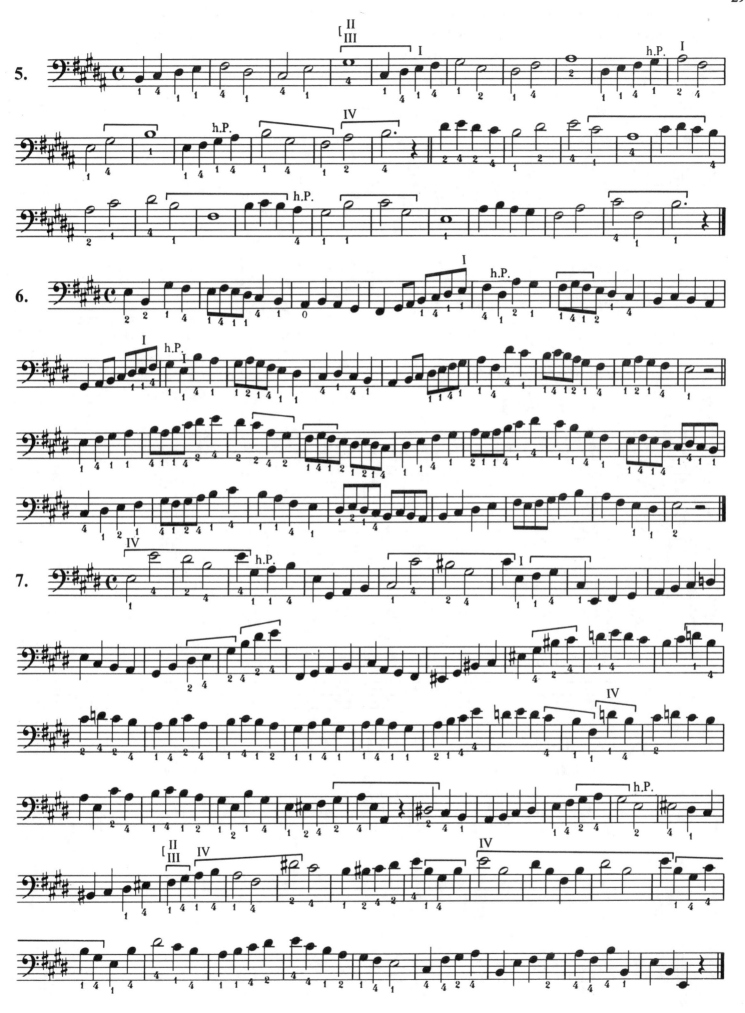

The V. Position

lies one-half tone higher than the IV.
In this and the following two positions, the thumb, which so far was placed along the middle of the back of the neck, now changes this place, by gradually moving towards the left side of the neck.
The V. Position contains the following intervals:

ポジションV

ポジションVは、ポジションIVより半音高く位置する。
このポジションと、後の2つのポジションについては、ネックの裏側の中央部にあった親指がその位置を変え、順にネックの左はしの方へと移動して行く。ポジションVは、次の各音程を含む。

Exercises on the Separate Strings.

各弦ごとの練習

Exercises in the V. Position on all the Strings.

全ての弦上での
ポジションVの練習

**Exercises in the V. Position
together with the preceding Positions.**

F Major Scale. ｜ヘ長調音階

Intermediate Position between the V. and VI. Position.

This Position lies one-half tone higher than the V Position and contains the following intervals:

このポジションは、ポジションⅤより半音高く位置し、次の各音程を含む。

On the G String ｜G線上で　　　　　　　　　On the D String ｜D線上で

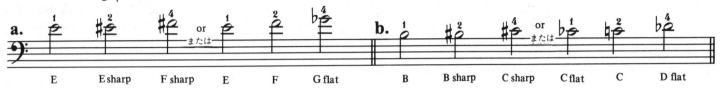

On the A String ｜A線上で　　　　　　　　　On the E String ｜E線上で

Exercises on the Separate Strings.

On the G String

On the D String

D線上で

On the A String

A線上で

On the E String

E線上で

Exercises between the V. and VI. Position. on all the Strings.

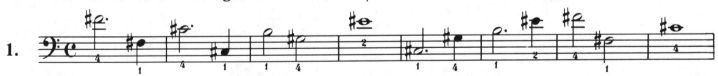

34

Exercises between the V. and VI. Positions together with the preceding Positions.

先行ポジションを伴う
ポジションⅤとⅥの間の練習

F sharp Major Scale ｜嬰ヘ長調音階

O492

6.

The VI. Position.

lies one whole tone higher than the V Position, or one-half tone higher than the preceding Intermediate Position.

In order to place the hand in as convenient and practical a position as possible, the short fourth finger is not used from this Position on, and the third finger is employed in its stead.

In this Position it is advisable to press the strings with the third finger only in *pizzicato* and *fortissimo* passages, as at this point the Octave (Harmonic) of the open string may be produced by merely touching the string. If the string is firmly pressed with the third finger, the latter must be supported by the first and second; however if the octave is taken as a harmonic, the first and second must be lightly raised. **36**

This Position contains the following intervals:

ポジションⅥ

ポジションⅥは、ポジションⅤより1音高く、また、先行する中間ポジションより半音高く位置する。

できるだけ都合よく実際的な位置に手を置くために、このポジションから先では短い第4指は用いられず、代わりに第3指が使用される。

このポジションにおいて、第3指で弦をおさえるのは、ただ「ピッツィカート」の時と、「フォルティッシモ」（すなわち強い音）のパッセージの時に限るのが当を得ており、開放弦のオクターヴ（ハーモニックス）の場合は、ただ単に弦に触れるのみでよい。もし弦が、第3指によってしっかりとおさえられれば、あとは第1、及び第2指によって補助される。しかし、もしオクターヴをハーモニックスとして生じさせたければ、第1及び第2指は軽くあげておく。**36**

このポジションは、次の各音程を含む。

Exercises on the Separate Strings.

各弦ごとの練習

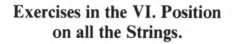

Exercises in the VI. Position on all the Strings.

全ての弦上での ポジションⅥの練習

Exercises in the VI. Position together with the preceding Positions.

先行ポジションを伴う
ポジションVIの練習

G Major Scale｜ト長調音階

O492

38

Intermediate Position between the VI. and VII. Positions.

This Intermediate Position lies one-half tone higher than the VI. Position and in playing upon the G and D strings the first, second and third fingers are also employed. But with the following difference: while the octave of the open string is produced in the VI. Position by simply touching the string with the third finger, in this Intermediate Position the string must be pressed down with the second finger, to avoid the sounding of the octave-harmonic of the open string as otherwise the latter will be heard, even if a note be taken somewhat higher or lower.

Through the wrong placing of the second finger however, the placing of the third finger might also become faulty. On the A string only the first and second finger can be used, as the length and strength of the third finger will not allow of its pressing this thick string upon the finger-board satisfactorily. The E string is not employed in this Intermediate Position. **40**

The thumb, which up to this time has been placed upon the left side of the neck, is now moved to the side of the finger-board in the same position. **41**

It must be observed that this and the following Position may also be played in the "Thumb position"; but I would advise the student to master the fingering of this Intermediate Position, as he is apt to meet with quick passages between the VI. and VII. Position which would be extremely difficult or entirely impossible if executed from the VI. to the Thumb-position.

The following intervals occur in this Intermediate Position:

ポジションⅥとⅦの間の
中間ポジション

この中間ポジションは、ポジションⅥより半音高く位置し、G線及びD線上で第1、第2、第3指を用いて演奏される。しかし、次の場合は異なる：第3指により、軽く弦を触れただけでポジションⅥにおいて生ずる開放弦のオクターヴに対し、この中間ポジションでは、特に、第2指はしっかりとおさえなければならない。それは、たとえ音符がいくぶん高め、または低めであっても（軽くおさえていると）聞こえてしまう開放弦のオクターヴ（ハーモニックス）という不必要な音を避るためである。

第2指の不正確な配置は、第3指の配置をも過まらせる。A線上においては、第1及び第2指のみが用いられ、指板上のこの太い線をおさえるのに、第3指の長さと、力の強さは不適当である。この中間ポジションでは、E線は用いられない。**40**

この場合、親指はネックの左側に置かれ、同じポジションのまま、指板の側面へと移動される。**41**

このポジション及び次のポジションでも、「親指のポジション」で演奏されることが守られなければならない。しかし、私は学習者がこの中間ポジションの運指を習得するに際し、ポジションⅥとⅦの間で、速く、大変に難しい動きや、もしポジションⅥから親指のポジションへと弾く場合の、ほとんど不可能な動きなどに出くわすことがよくあることを忠告しておきたい。

次の各音程は、この中間ポジションの内で生ずる。

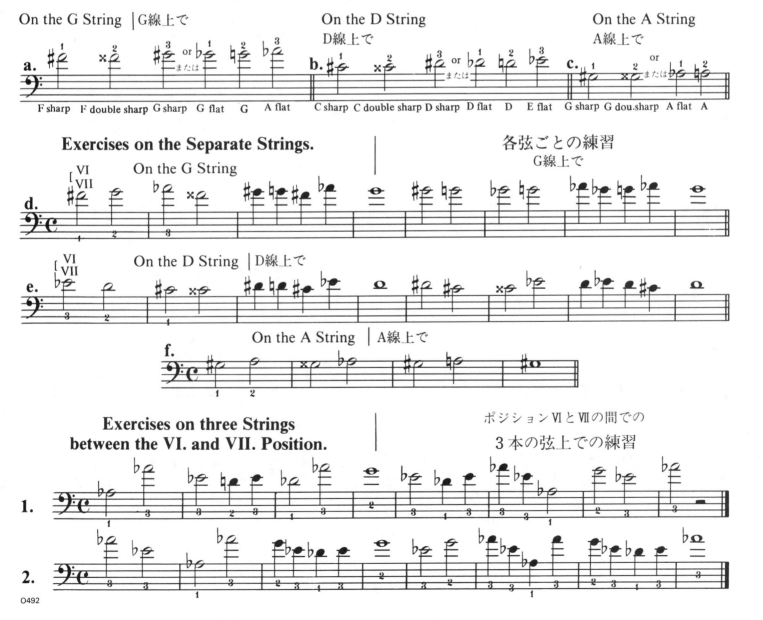

On the G String | G線上で

On the D String | D線上で

On the A String | A線上で

Exercises on the Separate Strings. | 各弦ごとの練習

Exercises on three Strings between the VI. and VII. Position. | ポジションⅥとⅦの間での **3本の弦上での練習**

Exercises between the VI. and VII. Position together with all the preceding Positions.

全ての先行ポジションを伴う
ポジションⅥとⅦの間の練習

A flat Major Scale | 変イ長調音階

41

6.

O492

The VII. Position

lies one whole tone higher than the VI. Position, or one-half tone higher than the preceding Intermediate Position.

As in the preceding Position the first, second and third finger is employed upon the *G* string and only the first and second finger for the *D* and *A* string, as the third finger is not of sufficient length to produce the notes correctly. The octave of the open string, which could also be taken as a harmonic in this Position, must be pressed against the finger-board in this instance by the first finger, in order that the second and third fingers may produce their respective intervals clearly and with precision **43**

The following intervals occur in this Position:

ポジションVII

ポジションVIIは、ホジションVIより1音高く位置し、先行する中間ポジションより半音高い。

先行ポジションにおいては、G線上で第1、第2、第3指が用いられ、D線及びA線上では、第3指は正確な音を出すために適した長さを持たないので、第1と第2指のみが用いられる。開放弦によるオクターヴ、またはこのポジションで得られるハーモニックスは、第2及び第3指が各々の音程を明確かつ正確に出せるようにするために、第1指により指板をおさえなければならない。**43**

次の各音程は、このホジションの内に生ずる。

2.

A Major Scale │ イ長調音階

3.

To complete the list of all the *Major Scales* the student needs only three more which, if subjected to an enharmonic change, have already been played; namely the *C sharp Major scale* which is played with the same fingering as the *D flat Major*, *G flat Major* like *F sharp Major*, and *C flat Major* like *B Major*.

全ての長音階の一覧を満たすために、学習者は異名同音の考え方に基づけば、すでに弾いたことのある次の3つを付加すれば足りる。すなわち、嬰ハ長調の音階は、変ニ長調の音階と同じ運指であり、同様に、変ト長調は嬰ヘ長調と、変ハ長調は口長調と同じである。

44

C sharp Major Scale｜嬰ハ長調音階

Exercise
練習

G flat Major Scale｜変ト長調音階

Exercise
練習

C flat Major Scale｜変ハ長調音階

Exercise
練習

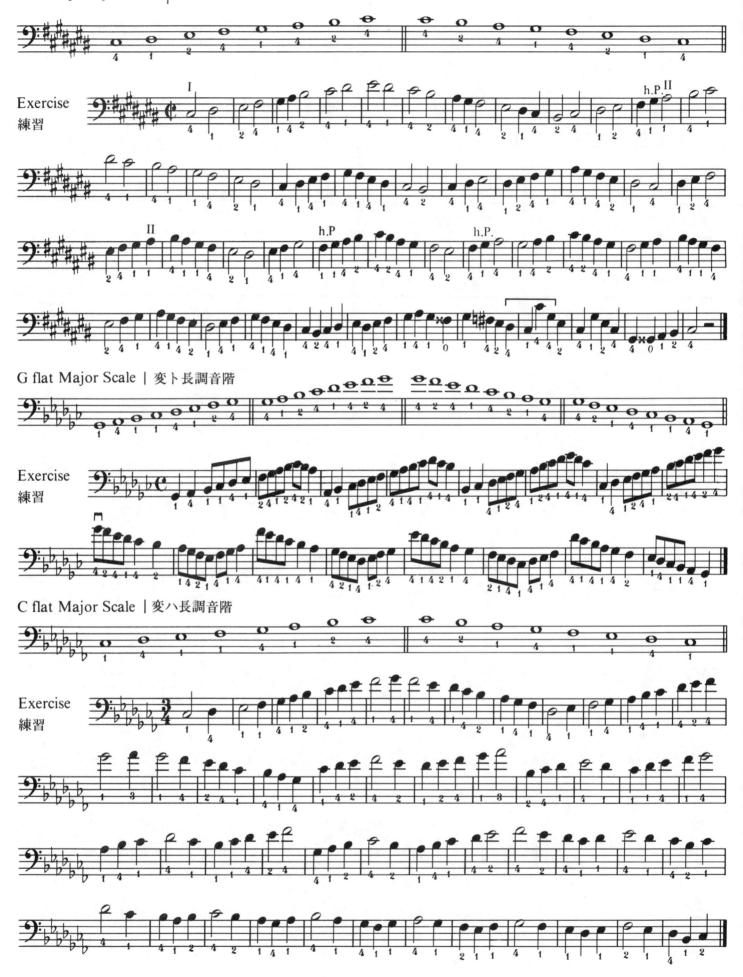

O492

45

Part II.
Minor Scale and Exercises.

第II部
短調の音階と練習

O492

B Minor
ロ短調

Exercise 3
練習

F sharp Minor
嬰ヘ短調

Exercise 4
練習

C sharp Minor
嬰ハ短調

Exercise
練習

D Minor
ニ短調

Exercise
練習

etc.

D

48

G Minor
ト短調

Exercise
練習

C Minor
ハ短調

Exercise
練習

F Minor
ヘ短調

Exercise
練習

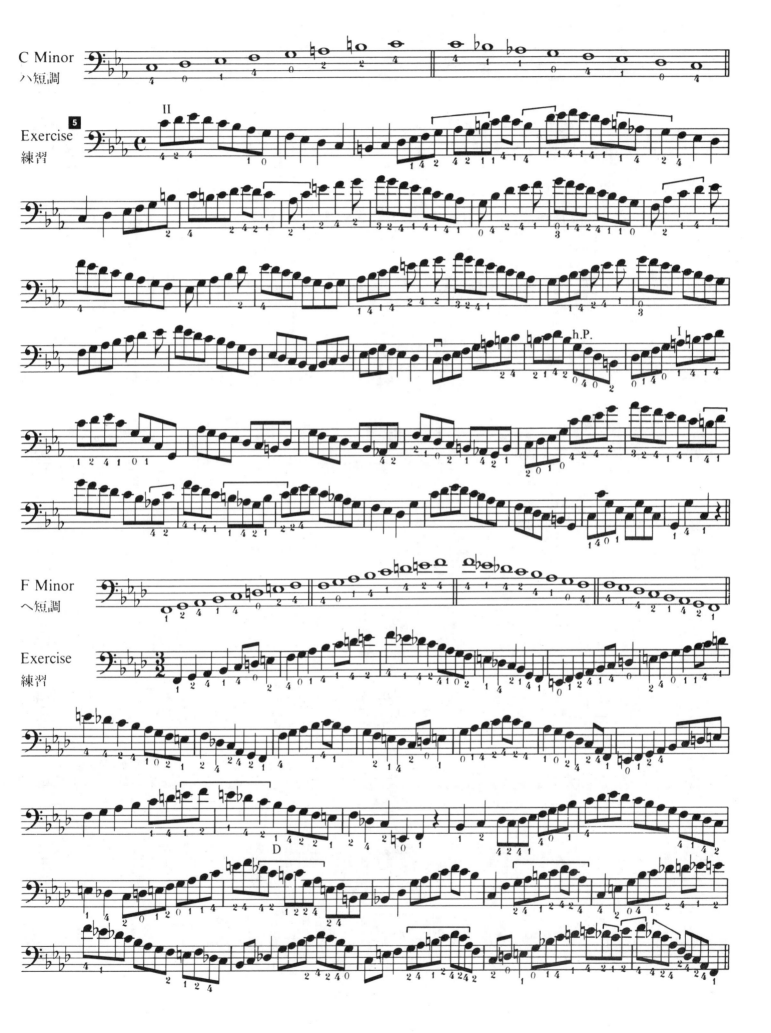

Enharmonic Minor Scales.　　異名同音による短調の各音階

B flat Minor
変ロ短調

Exercise
練習

The A sharp Minor Scale is played with the same fingering as the B flat Minor Scale.
嬰イ短調の音階は、変ロ短調の音階と同じ運指によって演奏される。

Exercise
練習

51

E flat Minor
変ホ短調

Exercise
練習

D sharp Minor is played like E flat Minor.
嬰ニ短調は変ホ短調と同じように演奏される。

Exercise
練習

O492

52

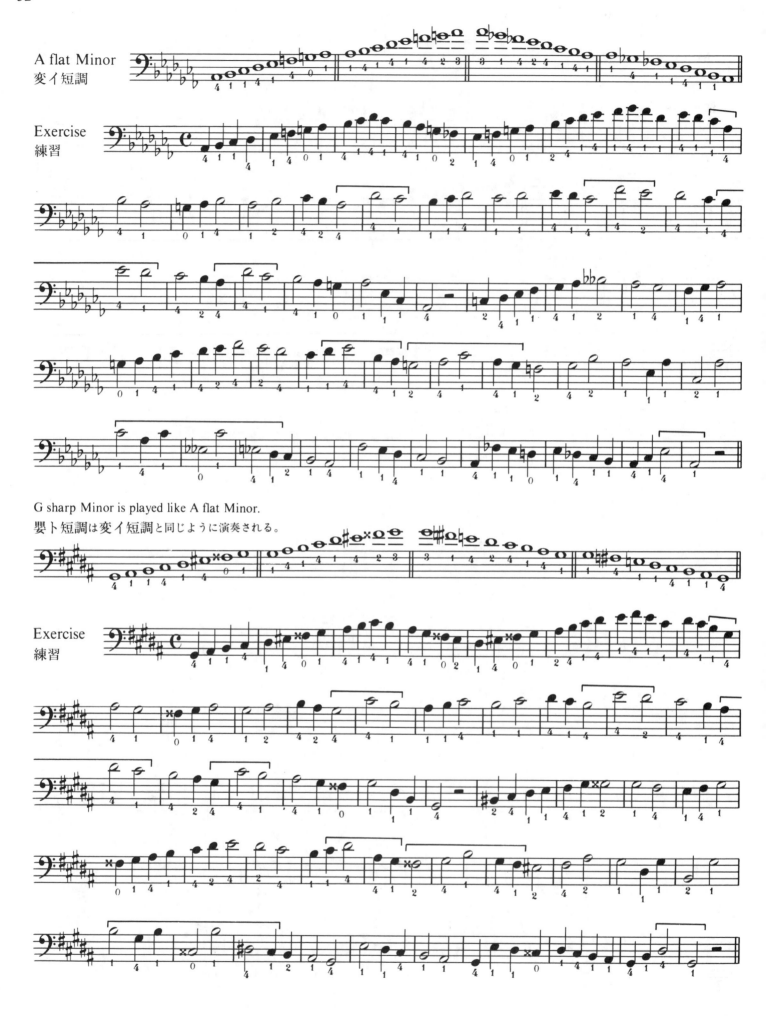

A flat Minor
変イ短調

Exercise
練習

G sharp Minor is played like A flat Minor.
嬰ト短調は変イ短調と同じように演奏される。

Exercise
練習

Intervals and Exercises. 音程と練習

Thirds
3度

54

O492

Exercises. 練習

56

Fourths. 4度

57

O492

58

Exercise in Fourths. 　　　　　４度の練習

O492

Fifths. [11]　　　　　　　　　　　　5度 [11]

60

O492

Exercise in Fifths.　　　　　　5度の練習

Sixths.

It must be observed that with all intervals played across three strings, the lower note must be taken with the Up-Bow, in lively tempos. **12**

6度

全ての6度音程は、3本の弦を横切って（ただし真中の弦は使用されない）演奏され、低い方の音は、活々としたテンポの上げ弓で弾かれなければならない。**12**

63

O492

Exercise in Sixths.   6度の練習

Sevenths.   7度

66

Exercise in Sevenths. 7度の練習

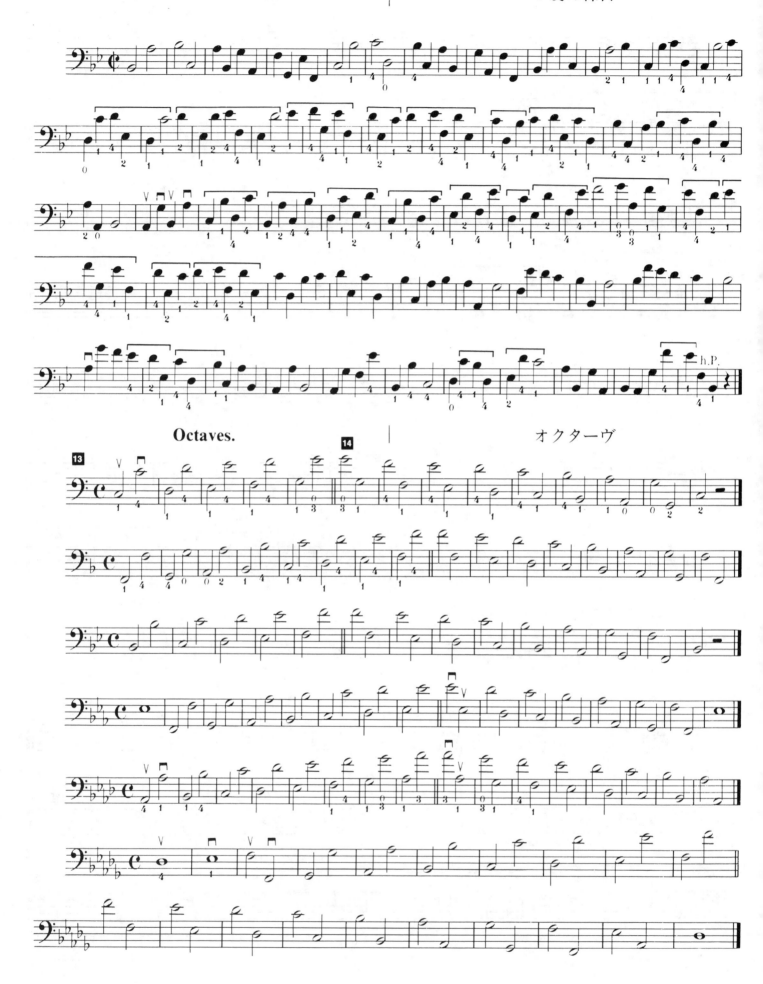

Octaves. オクターヴ

Exercise in Octaves. オクターヴの練習

Part III.
Explanatory Remarks as to the most important signs of expression.

As a rule every tone is sustained exactly as long as the value of the note calls for. However, the necessity to deviate from this rule arises in such cases where the original value of a note is increased or decreased through certain signs of expression. The most important of these signs for a string instrument player, are such as indicated: *Staccato, Legato,* and *Portamento* or *Appogiato Bowing.*

Staccato

means "detached" and indicates that the notes are to be played shorter than their original value calls for. Staccato is usually indicated by dots, or if the notes are to be played exceedingly short, by small, solid, vertical wedges above the notes. In the latter case it is designated as *Staccatissimo.*

第III部
最も重要な表現記号に関する注意説明

原則として全ての音はその音符の音価を正確な長さで保持しなければならない。しかし、この原則から逸脱しなければならない場合として、1つの音符に対し、ある表現記号が加えられることにより、もとの音価が増減されることが起る。弦楽器奏者にとってこれらの記号の最も重要なものは、**スタッカート、レガート、ポルタメント**または**アッポジャート・ボーイング**などの表示である。

スタッカート

スタッカートは、「切り離した」という意味であり、これが記された音符は、もとの音価より短く演奏される。スタッカートは通常、点によって表示される。また、音符上に小さな垂直の「クサビ形」の点が付され、非常に短く演奏される場合は、**スタッカティッシモ**と呼ばれる。

Manner of indicating the Staccato:
スタッカートの記法：

Execution:
奏法.

Manner of indicating the Staccatissimo:
スタッカティッシモの記法：

Execution:
奏法：

Legato

means "tied" and indicates that the notes are to played for their full value and in such a sustained manner, that each note is connected with the next following one as closely as possible. In addition to the word *Legato* itself, this style of bowing is indicated by a slur ⌒, connecting or embracing the notes to be tied. Notes marked with such a slur ⌒ are always played in one bow.

for instance:

レガート

レガートは、「結ばれた」という意味で、各音符は、その音価全部を充分に維持しながら次に続く音との間を可能な限り切らずに演奏される。レガートの語に対する付加として、このボーイング方式は、スラー ⌒ によって表示され、各音符はスラーで連結もしくは囲むことにより結ばれる。

このようなスラー ⌒ によって記された各音符は、常に一弓で弾かれる。

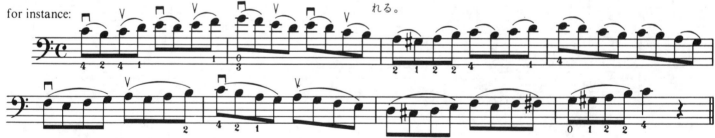

An exception may be made in the case of a longer *forte* passage; here it is necessary to change the bow in order to preserve the strength of the passage; however, this must be done in such a way that the passage will not be disconnected too obviously.

長い、**フォルテ**のパッセージの場合は除外される。この場合、パッセージの力強さを保持するために、替え弓が必要である。しかし当然のことながら、そのパッセージは、とぎれとぎれになってはならない。

Portamento or Appogiato [1]

means "sustained" and designates a combination of *Staccato* and *Legato* bowing. The indication consists of little lines placed above the notes, the lines being connected by a slur.

ポルタメントまたはアッポジャート [1]

アッポジャートは、「保持して」という意味で、スタッカートとレガートのボーイングのコンビネーションによるものである。表示は、音符上の小さな横線と、スラーの両者で構成される。

While such notes, supplied with *Appogiato signs* are played in a detached manner, they must nevertheless be produced very softly and played in one bow.

このようなアッポジャート記号が付された音符の状態では、大変に柔らかく、しかも一弓で弾かれるにもかかわらず、デタッシェ奏法で演奏される。

Varieties of Bowing. | 様々なボーイング

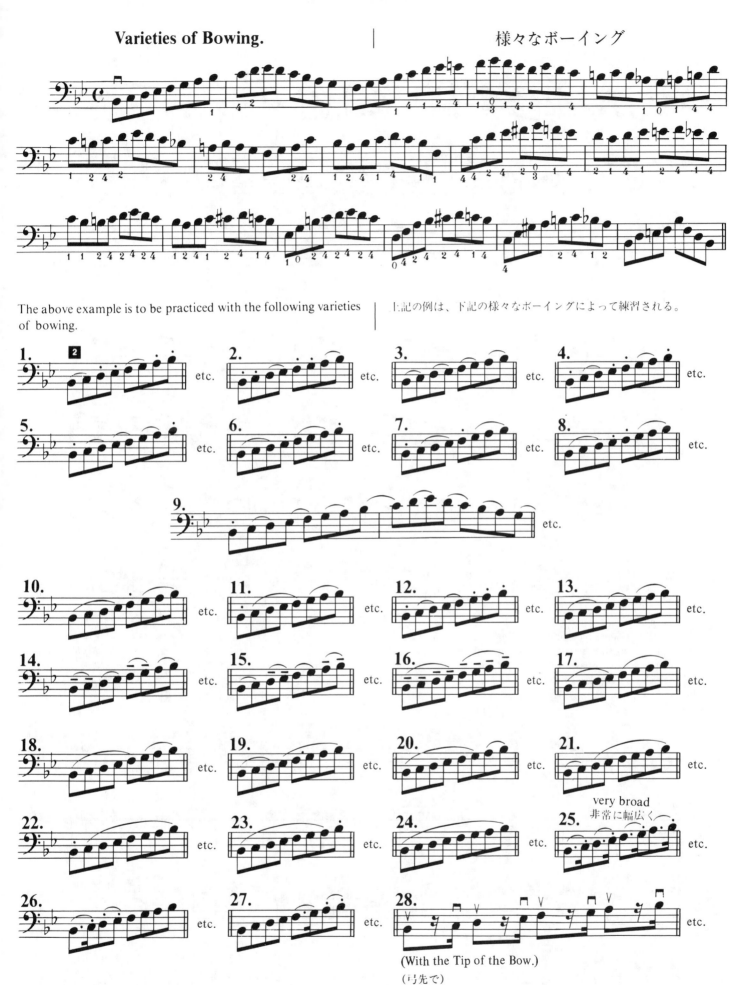

The above example is to be practiced with the following varieties of bowing. | 上記の例は、下記の様々なボーイングによって練習される。

very broad
非常に幅広く

(With the Tip of the Bow.)
（弓先で）

Triplet — Bowings.　　　　　3連音のボーイング

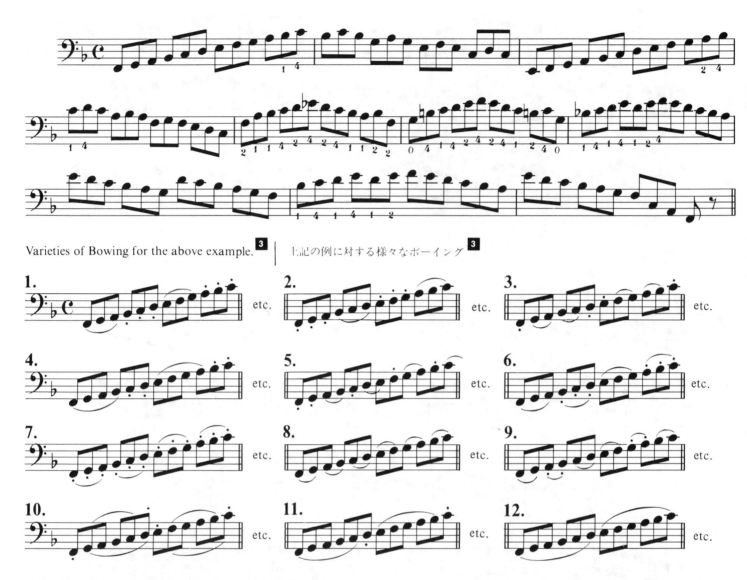

Varieties of Bowing for the above example. **3**　　上記の例に対する様々なボーイング **3**

In case of dotted passages or where the individual dots are replaced by pauses, as shown in the following examples a, b, c, d, e the two first notes must invariably be played with the Down and the third with the Up-stroke; this must be specially observed and taken heed of in quick tempos. **4**

スタッカートによるパッセージ、または個々のスタッカート音は、休止符によって置き換えられる。次の a、b、c、d、e に見られる例では、最初の2つの音符は一定に下げ弓で演奏され、3番目の音符は上げ弓で演奏される。このことは特に守らなければならないし、また、速いテンポにおいては注意を要する。 **4**

72

But in case of such a passage like the following the first note must be played with the Down; and the two following ones with the Up-Bow:

しかし、次のパッセージのような場合、最初の音符は下げ弓で、次の２つの音符は上げ弓で演奏される。

or this: —

or this: —

or this: —

or this: —

or this: —

1.

Special division of the bow is necessary for particular passages in order to execute them clearly and with exact rhythm. In order to provide the student with a guide in this direction, the following examples, with carefully marked bowings, have been added. **5**

特定のパッセージにおいては、正確なリズムで明確な演奏をするために、特に注意深い弓の配分が必要である。学習者に対して、この方式を紹介するために、以下の例で注意深くボーイング記号を記す。 **5**

1.

74

In slow tempo and "forte" the above exercise would be played with the following bowing.

上記の練習曲は、下記のボーイングにより、ゆっくりしたテンポで、かつ「フォルテ」で弾く。

Slowly ｜ ゆっくり

In quick tempo and "piano" the above exercise would be played with the following bowing.

上記の練習曲は、下記のボーイングにより、早いテンポで、かつ「ピアノ」で弾く。

15.

As it is impossible to describe the exact bowing of every passage we are apt to meet, the student will do well to remember that he is to begin with *the Down Bow* when

 1. a passage starts with the *full bar* and
 2. when one or more notes are *slurred* together and occur on the *first* beat or on any one of the *heavy beats* of a bar.

However the *Up beat* of a bar, if it is made up of *one* or *several detached notes of uneven number,* is always played with the *Up Bow*; this is also done in bars in which the notes will bring about an uneven number of bowings.

In case of *longer* and *uniform* passages the *heavy beats* of a bar are always played with the *Down* and the *light ones* with the *Up Bow.* **8**

As already observed in the case of *Sixths* an exception must be made in such passages, which are played across two strings in quick tempo; in such cases it is absolutely necessary to use the opposite bowing.

全てのパッセージについて正確なボーイングを詳述することは不可能である。そこで学習者は、次のことをよく記憶しておくべきである。

 1. あるパッセージが、**小節の頭から休止符を置かれることなく始められる場合。**及び、
 2. 1つ、またはそれ以上の音符が、共に**スラー**で連結され、それが小節の**第1拍目**、もしくは強拍部から始められている場合には、**下げ弓**で開始する。

しかし、ある小節の弱拍部が、**1つ**、もしくは幾つかの、一様でない数からなる**デタッシェ音**によって形成されている場合は、常に上げ弓で弾かれ、これはまた、各音符が引き起す一様でない数のボーイングによる各小節においても実施される。

長く、かつ均一のパッセージの場合は、小節の**強拍は常に下げ弓**で、**弱拍は上げ弓**で演奏される。**8**

すでに**6度**の場合に述べられた例外は、速いテンポにより、2本の弦を横切って弾かれるパッセージでも実施されなければならない。すなわち、このような場合は、反対のボーイングの使用が明らかに必要とされる。

Tremolo

is a quivering and rapid movement upon one and the same tone, and is produced by repeating the note with greatest speed for its entire time value.

Tremolo-bowing is indicated by the abbreviated word *trem.* or by the triple-crossed stems of the notes, as shown below.
The *Tremolo* is executed with the middle of the bow, and the movement must be brought about solely through the wrist. **9**

トレモロ

　トレモロは、同一の1音上での速い動きを伴う震動であり、その全音価に対して1つの音を、急速に反復させることによって得られるものである。
　トレモロ・ボーングは、*trem.* の省略文字、または下記に見られるように、符尾に交差された3本の線によって表示される。
　トレモロは、弓の中間部分で演奏され、手首の動きを通じてのみ生じさせられる。**9**

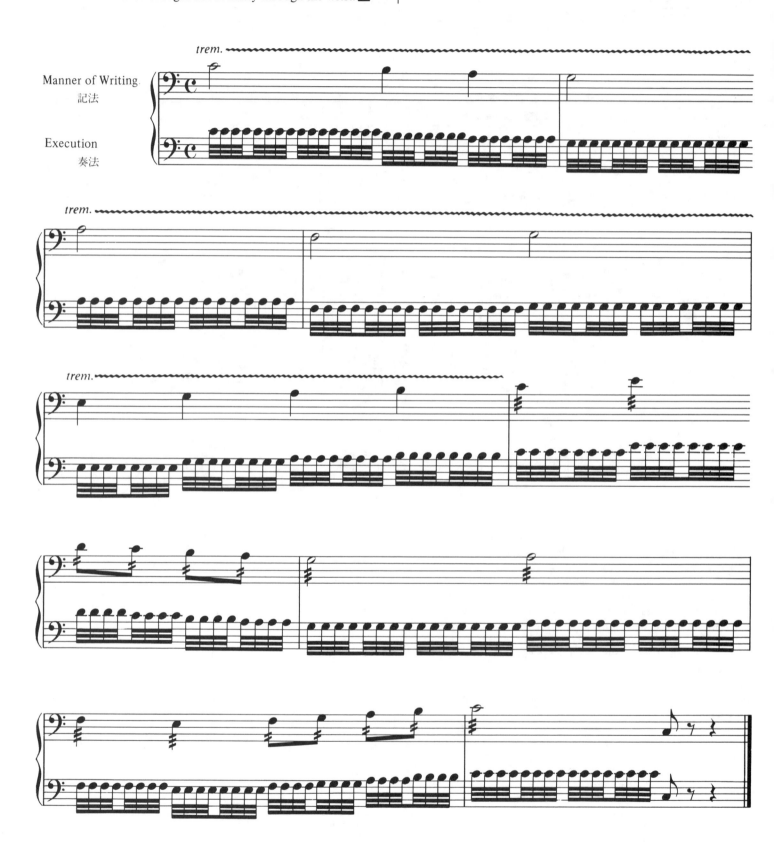

Pizzicato

(abbreviated *pizz.*) means, that instead of setting the strings into vibration with the bow, they should be plucked by a finger of the right hand.

In this case the bow is allowed to hang in a downward direction, being held by the fourth and little finger (inside the nut), and while the thumb is placed at the edge of the middle of the finger-board, the fore and middle fingers are held above the strings and employed for the *pizzicato*.

The strings are picked in the direction from left to right. In *piano* and *mezzoforte* passages, either the fore or middle finger may be used; but for *forte* passages both are employed, the right hand being moved nearer to the saddle whereever the force and strength of the *forte* is to be increased.

For *pizzicato* passages in quick tempo, the fore and middle finger should be employed alternately. With the term "*col arco*" the bow is again brought into use. **10**

ピッツィカート

ピッツィカート（省略文字は *pizz*）は、弓で弦を振動させる代わりに、右手の指で、かき鳴らすことを意味する。

この場合弓は、（毛箱の内側を）薬指と小指でひっかけて下向きにして持ち、親指は指板中央の側面に置き、人差し指と中指は、弦の上へもってきてピッツィカートのために用いられる。

弦は、左から右へとひき鳴らされる。「ピアノ」と「メッゾフォルテ」のパッセージの時は、人差し指か、中指が使われるが、「フォルテ」のパッセージでは両指が用いられる。そして、「フォルテ」の勢いと強さを増す時には、右手を上駒の方へ近づける。

速いテンポのピッツィカート・パッセージのためには、人差し指と中指を交互に使用する。"*col arco*"（コル・アルコ）の記号で、弓は再び使用される。**10**

Exercises. / 練習

80

Col Legno [12]

means, that instead of playing with the hair, the strings should be struck with the stick of the bow; in doing so the right hand, holding the bow, must be slightly turned towards the player.
"Col arco" indicates the usual manner of playing again.

コル・レーニョ [12]

コル・レーニョは、弓の毛の方で弾く代わりに、「さお」の側で弦をたたくことを意味し、右手で弓を持ち、わずかに奏者の方へ傾けなければならない。
"Col arco"（コル・アルコ）は、再び普通の演奏法でということを示す。

Exercise. / 練習

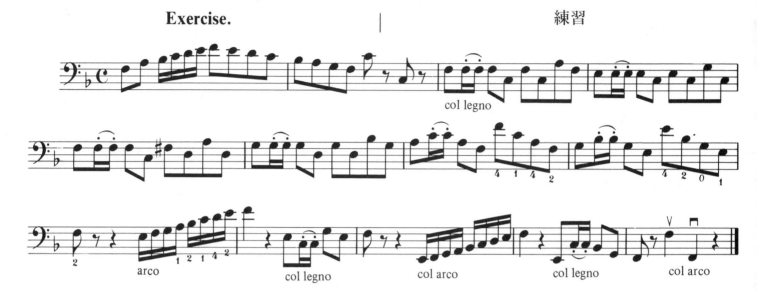

Ponticello. [13]

For the term "ponticello" or "sul ponticello" indicating that the original sound of the instrument should be changed, the playing is done with light bowing near to the bridge.

"Naturel" or "son naturel" indicates the natural sound of the instrument again.

ポンティチェルロ [13]

"ponticello"（ポンティチェルロ）、または "sul ponticello"（スル・ポンティチェルロ）の表示では、駒の近くを軽いボーイングでこすることにより、楽器本来の音色が変化させられる。
"Naturel"（ナチュレル）、または "son naturel"（ソン・ナチュレル）は、再び楽器本来の音色で、ということを示す。

Exercise. / 練習

O492

Chromatic Scales.

These are to be practiced at first detached and in slow tempo, later on slurred and in quicker tempo.

半音階

これらは、初めはゆっくりしたテンポのデタッシェで、後に、より速いテンポのスラーで練習される。

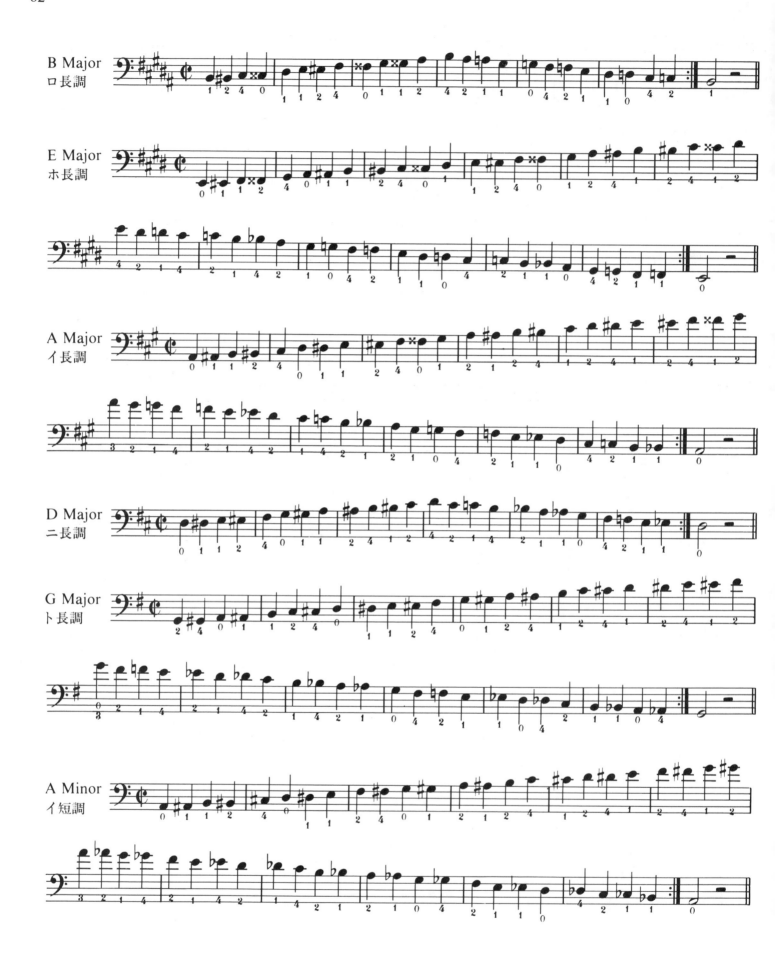

85

O492

86

Staccato Exercises.

When a number of detached *(staccato)* notes are played in one bow, the latter must be firmly set upon the strings, and the short strokes must be executed only with the wrist. The following examples should be practiced in slow tempo at first, and gradually with increased speed. **14**

スタッカート練習

　沢山のデタッシェ（スタッカート）音符が一弓で弾かれる場合、弓は常にしっかりと弦に密着していけなければならず、その短い拍動は、手首でもって弾かなければならない。次の各例は、初めはゆっくりしたテンポで、そして段階的に速度を増して行かなければならない。**14**

88

The Jumping Bow.

With this style of bowing, the bow leaves the string for a moment between each note. In order to avoid any roughness of tone, the playing should be done only with the wrist and with the middle part of the bow, which, in falling slightly touches the string. **15**

はね弓

この様式によるボーイングでは、弓は各音符の間で一瞬、弦を離れる。耳ざわりなどのような音をも避けるために、演奏は手首だけを用いて、弓の中央部分が弦に軽く落ちて触れるようにされなければならない。**15**

Exercises.

練習

The following exercise is to be practiced slowly and with short detached strokes at first; then gradually quicker and with a jumping bow.

次の練習は、初めはゆっくりと、しかも短いデダッシェの拍動で練習されなければならず、段階的により速く、そしてはね弓を使って実施されなければならない。

Part IV.
The Grace Notes
The long and short Appoggiatura,
the Double Grace Note, the Gruppetto,
the After-Beat, the Turn or Mordent,
the Inverted Mordent and the Trill.

1.) The Single Grace Note or Appoggiatura

is indicated by a small note. If its stem is not crossed by a little line, it claims half the time-value of the following principal note, is slurred to the latter in one bow and is named "long" Grace Note or Appoggiatura, for instance:

第Ⅳ部
装飾音
長・短・前打音、二重装飾音、グルペット、
後打音、ターン、モルデントとトリル。
1.) 単一な装飾音または前打音
単一な装飾音または前打音は、小音符で表示される。もし、その符尾に小さな線が交差されていなければ、次にくる主たる音符の半分の音価に値し、一弓のスラーで次の音へ進み、「長い」装飾音または前打音と呼ばれる。（譜例参照）

If the Grace Note is placed before a dotted note, it claims two-thirds of the time-value of the latter, for instance:

もし、装飾音が付点音符の前に置かれた場合は、後者の3分の2の音価に値する。（譜例参照）

The little Grace Note is played short and quickly and tied to the next note, if its stem is crossed by a little line; in this case it is named "short" Grace Note or Appoggiatura, for instance:

もし、小さな装飾音の符尾に小さな線が交差されていたら、それは短く、素早く、そして次の音符へつなげて演奏される。このような場合は、「短い」装飾音または前打音と呼ばれる。（譜例参照）

2.) The Double-Grace Note

differs from the single one in-so-far that, as its name implies, it consists of two notes. However, as the principal note must be played upon an exact part of the bar, the preceding note or pause looses as much of its own time-value, as the execution of the grace notes necessitates.

2.) 二重装飾音
二重装飾音は、その名が示すように2つの音符を含む限りにおいて、単一のそれと区別される。しかし主たる音符は、その小節内の正確な拍の位置で演奏されなければならないのであって、装飾音の演奏の必然性として、先行音符もしくは休止符それ自体の音価分は無視せざるを得ない。

3.) The Gruppetto

If more than two Grace Notes precede a note, the ornament is designated as a "Gruppetto." For instance:

3.) グルペット

もし、2つより多くの装飾音が1つの音符に先行している場合は装飾音は「グルペット」と名付けられる。（譜例参照）

Manner of Writing:
記法

Execution:
奏法

Exercise in Double Grace Notes and Gruppettos.

二重装飾音とグルペットの練習

Manner of Writing:
記法

Execution:
奏法

O492

4.) The After-Beat.

One or more Grace Notes may follow the principal note, the latter loosing as much of its time-value, as the execution of the After-Beat necessitates. As with the preceding Grace Note, the After-Beat is also tied to the principal note, for instance:

4.）後打音

1つ、もしくはそれ以上の装飾音が主たる音符に続く場合は、後打音の演奏の必然性として、後者の音価分は無視せざるを得ない。先行装飾音のように、この後打音も主たる音符にスラーで連結される。（譜例参照）

Manner of Writing:
記法

Execution:
奏法

a.

c.

5.) The Turn

consists of one principal note and two melodic auxiliary notes of which one is placed one step before and higher, and the other one step after and lower, than the principal note. But the opposite case may occur, namely: that the first auxiliary note may be lower and the second higher, the different execution being indicated by a special sign. If the Turn is to begin with the Upper Auxiliary note its execution is designated by the sign ∽ and known as a "Turn from Above." If it begins with the Lower Auxiliary note it is designated by the sign ∾ and known as a "Turn from Below." As shown in the following examples the Turn may be executed in various' ways, always remembering that every Turn must be played upon one string and in one bow. The simple Turn is made up of one principal note, preceded by three Grace Notes, the latter beginning either with the higher or lower auxiliary tone, for instance:

5.）ターン

ターンは、1つの主たる音と2つの旋律的補助音、つまり1つは、主たる音に先行する1音高い音と、もう1つは、後続する1音低い音によって構成される。しかし反対の場合も起る。すなわち：特別な記号によって表示され、異った演奏がなされる、先行補助音が低く、後続音が高い場合である。もし、ターンを上方補助音によって始めるときは、その演奏は∽記号で表示され、「上からのターン」として知られている。もし、ターンを下方補助音によって始めるときは、その演奏は∾記号で表示され、「下からのターン」として知られている。以下の例に示すように、ターンは様々な方法によって演奏され、それは常に1本の弦上で、一弓によって弾かれることを注意しておく。単一のターンは、1つの主たる音符と、それに先行する上方または下方補助音のどちらかで開始される3つの装飾音とによって構成される。（譜例参照）

Manner of indicating the Turn from above:
上からのターンの記法

Execution:
奏法

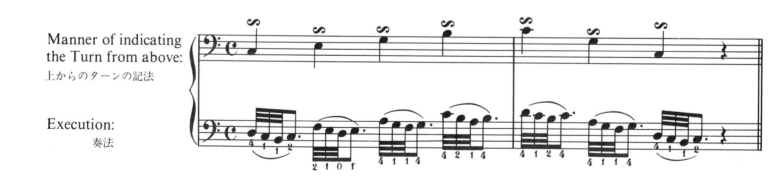

Manner of indicating the Turn from below:
下からのターンの記法

Execution:
奏法

Turns with Accidentals.

In case the upper or lower auxiliary tone is to be raised or lowered by an accidental, the respective signs are placed above or below the sign of the Turn, for instance:

臨時記号を伴ったターン

上方または下方補助音が、1つの臨時記号によって高められたり、低められたりする場合、各々の記号は、ターン記号の上または下に置かれる。

Turn Sign and Accidental as written for Raising the Lower Auxiliary Tone.

下方補助音を高めるために書かれた
ターン記号及び臨時記号

Manner of Writing: 記法

Execution: 奏法

Turn Sign and Accidental as written for Raising the Higher Auxiliary Tone.

上方補助音を高めるために書かれた
ターン記号及び臨時記号

Manner of Writing: 記法

Execution: 奏法

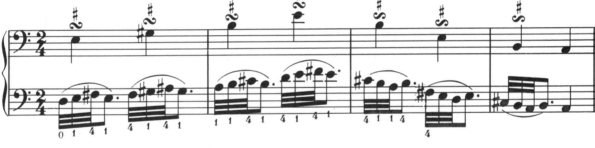

Turn Sign and Accidental as written for both Auxiliary Tones.

上方及び下方補助音のために書かれた
ターン記号及び臨時記号

Manner of Writing: 記法

Execution: 奏法

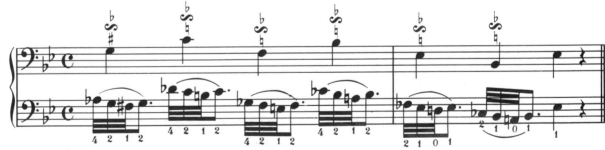

Turns between the Notes.

If a Turn is placed between two Principal notes it is played as long as possible after the first and shortly before the entrance of the second note, for instance:

2つの音符の間のターン記号

もし、ターンが2つの主たる音符の間に置かれた場合、最初の音符の後は、できるだけ長く、そして2つ目の音符に入る前は、より短く演奏する。

Manner of Writing: 記法

Execution: 奏法

If an additional grace note precedes the sign of the Turn, on the same degree as the principal note, for instance: | もし、ターン記号に先行して、付加の装飾音が主たる音符と同じ音高に置かれた場合 （譜例参照）：

it is played in this case, as follows.
このように演奏される。

If the sign of the Turn follows a dotted note, it is played shortly before the Dot and in such a way that the last note of the Turn is sustained for the entire time-value of the Dot, for instance: | もし、ターン記号が付点音符の後にきた場合、付点の付された音符は短く、そしてターンの終りの音は、完全に付点の音価分だけ保たせる。 （譜例参照） ：

Manner of Writing: 記法

Execution: 奏法

If the principal Note of the Turn is followed by two Dots: | もし、ターンの主たる音符が、二重付点の後に来た場合：

the execution is as follows. このように演奏される。

Exercise with Turns.
Slowly
ゆっくり

ターンの練習

Manner of Writing: 記法

Execution: 奏法

95

6.) The Mordent.

The Mordent begins with its principal note, adds a note on the neighboring higher or lower step and returns immediately to its principal note. Two kinds of signs are used for this group of grace notes; ⫶ for the one beginning with the upper auxiliary tone and ⫶ for the one beginning with the lower. In case of accidentals the respective sign is placed above the Mordent sign. The execution of the Mordent is always upon one string and in one bow.

6.) モルデント

モルデントは、その主たる音符から始まり、隣接する上方または下方音を加え、直ちにその主たる音符に戻る。2つの種類の記号が装飾音のこのグループに使用される：⫶は上方補助音を、⫶は下方補助音を伴って開始される。臨時記号各種は、モルデント記号の上方に置かれる。モルデントの演奏は、常に1本の弦上で、しかも一弓で行われる。

Manner of indicating the Mordent with the upper Auxiliary Tone.
上方補助音を伴うモルデントの記法

Indication with the Lower Auxiliary Tone.
下方補助音を伴う記法

Indication with Accidentals.
臨時記号を伴う記法

O492

Exercises for the Mordent.　モルデントの練習

7.) The Trill.

Trilling indicates the quick repetition of a principal note with its next-higher neighboring note, for the entire time-value of the principal note. It is indicated by the sign *tr* . The Trill can be executed either with a whole or half-tone, according to the requirements of any particular Key.

As a rule the Trill is commenced upon the principal note, and if not otherwise indicated the After-Beat is added after the last trill. This After-Beat is usually indicated by two small notes, the first one of which is one step lower than the principal note and the second one being the principal note itself. Short Trills, with their After-Beats, are played in one bow and with longer ones the bow should be changed as little as possible.

Trills of a Whole Tone.

To assure an even and clear execution, the trills should be practiced very slowly at first.

7.) トリル

トリルは、主たる音符とそれに隣接する上方音とで、主たる音符の全音価分だけ、速い速度により反復することを示す。それは、*tr.* の記号で表示される。トリルは、それ個有の調性の要求に従って、全音、または半音のいずれかの音程で演奏ができる。

原則として、トリルは主たる音符から始められ、もし記載がなければ、後打音が最後のトリルの後に付け加えられる。この後打音は、通常2つの小音符によって表示され、前者は主たる音符より1音低く、2番目は主たる音符自体である。後打音を伴う短いトリルは一弓で演奏され、長いそれでは最小限の替え弓が行われる。

全音程の継続するトリル

均一で明確な演奏を確立するために、トリルは初め、大変にゆっくりと練習しなければならない。

Manner of Writing:
記法

Execution:
奏法

Trills of a Half Tone.

半音程の継続するトリル

98

Trills beginning with the Upper Tone. ｜ 上方音により開始するトリル

Trills succeeded by an After-Beat. ｜ 後打音により終結されるトリル

Exercises for the Trill. トリルの練習

100

A number of trills following in close succession are termed a *"Chain of Trills"* and the "After-Beat" is added only after the last trill, for instance:

連続して沢山のトリルが続く場合は、「トリルの鎖」と呼ばれ、「後打音」は最後のトリルの後だけに付けられる。（譜例参照）

Exercise. 練習

Legato Exercises. [2]

With the following exercises specially designed for stretching and strengthening the fingers and for perseverance in playing, the student should pay careful attention to stretching his fingers as much as possible and particularly to that of the fourth finger.

To be practiced slowly and with detached bowing at first; then gradually quicker and slurred, as indicated by the different bowings numbered 1 and 2.

レガートの練習 [2]

指を伸ばしたり強化したりするために、そして忍耐強く演奏するために特別に書かれた次の各練習曲によって、学習者は各指を伸ばすことに、とりわけ第4指について、最大限の注意を払わなければならない。

初めはゆっくり、そしてデタッシェのボーイングで練習し、それから段階的に1と2で示された異なるボーイングによって、より速く、スラーで練習する。

Legato Exercises on two Strings.

Also to be practiced slowly at first, and gradually with increased speed. **4**

２本の弦上でのレガート練習

これらもまた、初めはゆっくりと、そして段階的に速度を増して練習する。**4**

Exercise in Broken Chords extending through all the Major Keys.

This exercise should also be practiced slowly and with detached bowing at first and gradually with increased speed and slurred bowing. **5**

全ての長調に拡大される

分散和音練習

この練習もまた、初めはゆっくりと、しかもデタッシェのボーイングで練習され、段階的に速度を増し、スラーのボーイングで実施される。**5**

106

On the Various Styles of Writing for the Double Bass.

Frequently, and especially with church music, the parts for Violoncello and Double Bass are written on one staff.

If written this way, both instruments will either play identical notes (*unisono*), in octaves, or one or the other will pause.

The following indications are used in such cases: if a passage is marked *Violoncell*, *senza Basso*, or *Basso tacet*, the Basses are to pause and re-enter at the places marked *Basso*, *col Basso*, or *tutti*, as shown in the folowing:

ダブル・ベースのための
様々な様式による書式で

しばしば、そして特に教会音楽では、チェロとダブル・ベースのパートは同一5線上に書かれている。

もし、このような方法で書かれている場合、両方の楽器は同一音（ウニーソノ）をオクターヴで弾くか、または片方が休むかのいずれかの方法で演奏される。

次の各表示は、そのような場合に用いられる：もし、あるパッセージに、*Violoncell, senza Basso* または *Bosso tacet* と記されていれば、ベースは休み、下記の例のように、*Basso, col Basso* または *tutti* と記るされた場所で、再び入る。

Extracts from Mozart's Requiem.

モーツァルトの「レクイエム」よりの抜粋

O492

It also happens that in writing the parts of the *Cellos* and *Basses* on one staff, the parts to be played by the *Cello* alone, are written in the *Tenor clef*, and whereever the *Basses* are to join, the *Bass clef* is again employed, for instance:

チェロとベースのパートが同一5線上に書かれている場合、テナー記号で書かれた部分はチェロだけで弾かれ、ベースが加わる部分では、低音部記号が再び用いられる。（譜例参照）

Extract from Mozart's Requiem.

モーツァルトの「レクイエム」よりの抜粋

However there are exceptions to this rule, as shown in the following extract *"Quam olim"* from Mozart's Requiem. The eighth bar contains notes in the Bass clef which must still be played by the Cellos, the Basses only playing where the word *Basso* indicates their entrance.

しかし、次の例で見られるモーツァルトのレクエイムよりの抜粋「主が、かってアブラハムに」のように、この原則が除外される場合がある。第8小節目は低音部記号が含まれているが、まだチェロだけで弾かれ、ベースはその入りを示す Basso の語の所でのみ弾く。

Quam olim.

「主が、かってアブラハムに」

Sometimes the notes for the Double Bass are also written in the Tenor Clef; however to avoid any mistakes the word *Basso* is usually added in such places, as illustrated by the following:

時として、ダブル・ベースのための音符はテナー記号でも書かれる。しかし、どのようなまちがえをも避けるために、次の例のような *Basso* の語が通常その場所に加えられる。

Extract from Beethoven's Ninth Symphony.

ベートーヴェンの「第9交響曲」よりの抜粋

If a staff contains two sets of notes, generally the lower one is intended for the Double Bass and the upper one for the Violoncello, as illustrated in the following extract from a Haydn Menuett. Frequently, *Cello* is written above the staff or *Basso* below the staff.

もし、次に示められたハイドンのメヌエットよりの抜粋のように、1つの5線上に2つのパートが含まれている場合は、下の方が通常ダブル・ベースを意図し、上の方がチェロである。しばしば、*Cello* の語が5線の上方に、*Basso* が下方に書かれている。

Extract from a Menuett by Haydn.

ハイドンの「メヌエット」よりの抜粋

However if the notes are to be reversed, *Basso* is placed above and *Cello* below the two sets of notes, for instance:

しかし、もし音符が入れ換われば、*Basso* は上方、そして *Cello* は2つのパートの下方に置かれる。（譜例参照）

109

Rests occuring below the notes are usually meant for the Double Basses, and the latter are only expected to enter again at the end of the pauses, as shown below.

If the rests are marked for the Cello, the Double Bass must play alone.

Extract from Beethoven's Symphony "Eroica"

ベートーヴェンの「英雄」交響曲よりの抜粋

O492

When two or more staffs are connected with brackets, the Double Bass must always play the notes of the lowest one, unless it is marked *Basso tacet* or *Celli Solo*. The term *Col Cello* indicates that the Double Bass is to continue playing the Cello part, for instance:

2段またはそれ以上の5線が、括弧で譜表にされている場合、ダブル・ベースは *Basso tacet* もしくは *Celli Solo* の記載がない限り、常に最も低い音符を演奏しなければならない。*Col Cello* の表示は、ダブル・ベースも、チェロのパートを弾き続けることを意味する。(譜例参照)

Extract from an Overture by Schumann.

シューマンの「序曲」からの抜粋

In many compositions we find, that when two sets of notes occur on one staff, or when they are placed upon two staffs connected by a bracket, that both parts must be played by the Double Basses. In such cases the following terms are employed: *Divisi, Bassi divisi* or *Bässe getheilt.*

多くの作品中に、ダブル・ベースによって演奏されるべき1つの5線上に生じる2つのパート、あるいは括弧によって譜表にされた2段の5線を見出す。このような場合、次のような用語が使用される：*Divisi, Bassi divisi* または *Bässe getheilt*。

In playing excerpts of important orchestral and solo passages for Double Bass, the student should not only observe technical difficulties, but also give careful attention to the dynamics, i.e. the expression and degree of power to be applied to a note or a group of notes. The importance of this has long been underestimated by young Bass players. The bowings and the true value of the notes and rests must also be given the same attention.

ダブル・ベースのための、オーケストラ作品や独奏曲から抜粋された重要なパッセージを演奏する際に、学習者は技術的な難しさだけでなく、強弱法についても注意を払わなければならない。すなわち、表現と、音符上または音群上に適応されるべき力の度合などについて。この重要性は、長いこと若いベース奏者に軽視されてきた。ボーイングと、音符及び休止符の正しい音価も、また同じく注意が払われねばならない。

The Marriage of Figaro
(Wolfgang Amadeus Mozart)

From the Overture.

フィガロの結婚
(ヴォルフガング・アマデーウス・モーツァルト)

序曲より

Allegro con brio and Finale
from Symphony No. 3 (Eroica)
(Ludwig van Beethoven)

アレグロ・コン・ブリオと終曲
交響曲第3番「英雄」より
(ルートヴィヒ・ヴァン・ベートーヴェン)

FINALE 終曲
Allegro molto (♩=76)

FUGUE フーガ

Presto (♪ = 116)

Andante con moto and Allegro
from Symphony No. 5
(Ludwig van Beethoven)

アンダンテ・コン・モートとアレグロ
交響曲第5番より
（ルートヴィヒ・ヴァン・ベートーヴェン）

Leonore Overture No. 3
from the Opera "Fidelio"
(Ludwig van Beethoven)

レオノーレ序曲第3番
オペラ「フィデリオ」より
（ルートヴィヒ・ヴァン・ベートーヴェン）

118

O492

Euryanthe Overture
(Carl Maria von Weber)

オイリアンテ序曲
（カルル・マリア・フォン・ヴェーバー）

Roman Carnival Overture
(Hector Berlioz)

ローマの謝肉祭序曲
（エクトル・ベルリオーズ）

etc.

Otello

(Giuseppe Verdi)
Bass Soli from Act IV **6**
Contrabassi soli con sordine
I soli Contrabassi a 4 Corde

オテロ
（ジュゼッペ・ヴェルディ）
第Ⅳ幕よりベース独奏 **6**
弱音器を付けたベース独奏
第Ⅰベースは、4弦楽器を使用

Poco più mosso (♩ = 80)

O492

Rigoletto
(Giuseppe Verdi)

Act. II. Duet for one Double Bass and one Cello, *con sordino.*

リゴレット
（ジュゼッペ・ヴェルディ）

第Ⅱ幕。弱音器を付けた、1台ずつのダブル・ベースとチェロのための2重奏。

Flying Dutchman
(Richard Wagner)

From the Overture

さまよえるオランダ人
（リヒャルト・ヴァーグナー）

序曲より

Allegro con brio

The Bartered Bride
(Friedrich Smetana)

From the Overture

売られた花嫁
（フリードリヒ・スメタナ）

序曲より

Academic Festival Overture
(Johannes Brahms)

大学祝典序曲
（ヨハネス・ブラームス）

L'istesso tempo, poco maestoso

Symphony No. 4, Op. 36
(Peter Ilyich Tchaikovsky)

交響曲 第４番 作品36
(ピョトル・イリイチ・チャイコフスキー)

Moderato con anima

FINALE 終曲
Allegro con fuoco

Symphony No. 6, Op. 74 (Pathétique)
(Peter Ilyich Tchaikovsky)

交響曲 第6番 作品74(悲愴)
(ピョトル・イリイチ・チャイコフスキー)

Allegro vivo

Marche Slave, Op. 31
(Peter Ilyich Tchaikovsky)

スラヴ行進曲 作品31
(ピョトル・イリイチ・チャイコフスキー)

Quintet
(Franz Schubert, Op. 114)

5重奏曲
（フランツ・シューベルト，作品114）

第III変奏曲
Var. III
Solo

第IV変奏曲
Var. IV

Jabberwocky *
from "Through the Looking Glass," Op. 36
(Deems Taylor)

ちんぷんかんぷん*
「鏡の中から」作品36より
（ディームズ・テイラー）

FUGA フーガ
Non troppo mosso, Tempo giusto

130

Part V.
The Recitative.

In accompanying the Recitative, the Double Bass player must 1.) follow the melody and the words of the singer; 2.) execute the bass notes of the respective chords clearly and with precision; 3.) not change the bow too often in sustained notes and 4.) constantly watch the musical director, especially in figured passages.

EXAMPLES.
Extract from "The Creation" by Haydn.

第 V 部

レシタティーヴ

レシタティーヴの伴奏では、ダブル・ベース奏者は、1.) 歌手の旋律と言葉に付き従わなければならず、2.) 各々の和音の低音を、明確かつ正確に演奏しなければならないし、3.) 保続された音符で、度々替え弓をしてはならず、4.)特に装飾されたパッセージにおいては、常に指揮者に注目していなければならない。

(例)
ハイドンの「天地創造」よりの抜粋

Geist Got - tes schweb-te auf der Flä - che der Was ser und Gott sprach: „Es wer-de

ウリエル
URIEL.

Licht" und es ward Licht. Und

pizz. f arco ff

Gott sah' das Licht, dass es gut war, und Gott schied das Licht von der Fin-ster-niss.

132

レシタティーヴ
Recitativ.

Andante

ウリエル
URIEL.

In vollem Glanze steig-et jetzt die Soñe strahlend auf

ein woñevoller Bräutigam   ein Riese stolz und froh   zu. rennen seine Bahn.

133

Mit leisem Gang und sanf - tem Schimmer schleicht der Mond die stil - le Nacht hin - durch

den aus-ge-dehnten Himelsraum ziert oh-ne Zahl der hellen Ster-ne Gold; und die Söh-ne Gott -es ver-

kündigten den vierten Tag, mit himlischem Ge-sang; seine Macht aus-rufend; Al-so!

O492

134

To complete my explanatory remarks relative to the Recitative, I will observe in particular, that this form of music is not only employed for singers, but also is often written for orchestral instruments as a solo. As an example, in Beethoven's Ninth Symphony the Recitatives are performed by the Cellos and Basses while the remainder of the orchestra joins in the accompaniment. As every Double Bass player is expected to know these particular Recitatives, I have thought it advisable to add them to this method, as follows:

レシタティーヴに関する私の注意説明を完璧にするために、私は特にこの音楽様式が声楽家のためだけでなく、オーケストラ楽器独奏のためにもしばしば用いられることについて述べよう。一例として、ベートーヴェンの第9交響曲のレシタティーヴでは、残りのオーケストラ・メンバーが伴奏部に加わっている間、チェロとベースによって演奏される。全てのダブル・ベース奏者は、このレシタティーヴの詳細について知りたいと願っているし、私もそれを以下のように、この教則本に付け加えることは当を得ていると考えた。

End of Book I.

After careful and thorough study of Book I of my Double Bass Method, the pupil is entirely prepared for Orchestral playing and in order to acquire the necessary practical routine, he should lose no opportunity for ensemble or orchestral experience.

Preparatory to proceeding to Book II of this Method, I would advise the pupil to study my *30 Etudes For the Acquisition of a Fine Tone and Rhythmic Surety* (Carl Fischer O2941) very thoroughly.

Franz Simandl

第1巻の終了

私のダブル・ベース教則本、第1巻を注意深く、かつ全体を通じて学習した後は、学習者はオーケストラ演奏のための完全な準備が備わり、つぎに必要な実際上の慣習を習得するためには、アンサンブルやオーケストラでの経験を積むために、どんな機会をものがすべきではない。

この教則本の第2巻に進む準備として、学習者は私の「良い音と確実なリズムを習得するための30の練習曲」（カール・フィッシャー版02941）を徹底的に学習するようにすすめたい。

フランツ・シマンドル

Commentary (Footnotes)

Part I.

Page 6

1 The teacher is encouraged to suggest additional rhythms for the bowing exercises on pages 6 and 7. For good tone production be careful to observe the placement, weight, speed and distribution of the bow as you practice.

Page 7

2 Many orchestral double bass parts of the late 19th century and especially the 20th century require the use of "thumb position". The student is encouraged to explore the entire range of the instrument through scales as soon as feasible without dividing the instrument into an "orchestral" range and a "solo" range.

Page 8

3 When vibrato is introduced at a later time, the position of the left hand is slightly altered.

Page 9

4 The teacher is encouraged to indicate the tempo (possibly using a metronome marking) and the amount of bow to be used in each exercise on this page and throughout the book.

Page 10

5 Refer to Preface to the 1984 Edition—Comment 2.

Page 11

6 When playing an open string move the entire left hand to the adjacent string to prepare for the following note.

7 When playing the low "G" on the "E" string, the open "G" should vibrate sympathetically.

Page 12

8 The student should be aware of the two-measure sequence in Exercise 4 and the four-measure sequence in Exercise 5.

Page 13

9 When shifting from first finger to first finger, the student should slide on the first finger and keep the string lightly pressed.

Fingers 2, 3 and 4 should remain close to the fingerboard.

Page 14

10 Refer to the Preface—Comment 5:

注　釈 （脚注）

第 I 部

6頁

1 教師には、6頁と7頁のボーイング練習について、様々なリズムを加えてみるようにすすめる。良い音を出すためには、練習にあたって弓の配置、重量、速度、そして弓の配分に注意をはらわなければならない。

7頁

2 19世紀後半と、特に20世紀におけるオーケストラのダブル・ベース・パートの多くは、「親指のポジション」の使用を要求する。学習者は、この楽器を「オーケストラ区分」と「独奏区分」という分け方をせずに、各音階を通じてすぐさま実施可能な全区分を調べてみるようにすすめる。

8頁

3 後にヴィブラートを導入する場合、左手の位置は多少変更される。

9頁

4 教師は（できるだけメトロノーム記号を用いて）テンポと、この頁および本書全体を通じての各練習曲に使用される弓の使用量についても、指示することをすすめる。

10頁

5 1984年版序文の第2項を参照。

11頁

6 開放弦での演奏の時は、次の音への準備のために、左手を完全に隣接した弦へ移動させること。

7 E線上での低い「ト音」の演奏に際し、開放のG線は共振する。

12頁

8 学習者は練習4においては2小節ごと、練習5においては4小節ごとの反復進行に気づくであろう。

13頁

9 第1指から第1指への移行に際して学習者は、弦を軽くおさえたまま、第1指をスライドさせる。第2、第3、第4指は指板近くに留まらせる。

14頁

10 序文、第5項を参照。

Page 15

11 Cross finger or prepare the "G" by placing fingers 2, 3 and 4 on the "D" string prior to playing "G" with the bow.

12 Prepare the "C♮" by placing the first finger on the "A" string before the "C♮" is played with the bow.

Page 16

13 An alternate bowing (lifting or recovering with two down bows) might be used as follows:

14 is an obsolete notation for and is rarely used— (likewise equals).

Page 19

15 Remember to keep the string lightly pressed when shifting.

16 *Shift on adjacent strings* (D♭ to E♭) — Begin the shift on the fourth finger "D♭" and slide on the "A" string to half position and at the same time move the first finger on the "D" string to "E♭".

17 *Shift on adjacent strings* (A♭ to G♭) — Begin the shift on the first finger "A♭" and slide on the "G" string to first position and at the same time move fingers 2, 3 and 4 on the "D" string to "G♭".

Page 20.

18 Remember to proportion the bow correctly.

Page 21.

19 Compare the intonation of these notes in octaves or in unison with the appropriate open string.

Page 22.

20 When playing the rhythm in measures 3 and 4, you may use a "Z" bowing. This means to use slightly more bow (with less weight) on the first down bow and less bow on the second and third quarter notes in measure 3 in order to have sufficient bow to play the half note in measure 4.

Page 23.

21 *Bow Compensation*:

  a. After the tied note  *recover* or *lift* the bow and place the bow *on the string* in the middle of the bow ready to play the next quarter note.

  b. Another way of compensating would be not to lift the bow, but to use a faster bow speed with less weight on the first up bow after the tied note.

22 During the quarter rest, move the bow in a downward direction above the string and place it on the string in the middle for the "C#".

Ex. etc.

23 Remember to proportion the bow.

15頁

11 指を交差させて、弓で「ト音」を弾くことに先立ち、「D線」上に第2、第3、第4指を置くことにより「ト音」の準備をする。

12 「ハ♮音」を弓で弾く前に、「A線」上で第1指により「ハ♮音」を準備する。

16頁

13 ボーイングの交替（浮かせて戻すか、または2つの下げ弓による新たな構えなおし）は、次のように使われる。

14 は. の古い書式で、めったに使われない。（ と とも同様である。）

19頁

15 移行中は、弦を軽くおさえておくことに注意する。

16 **隣接する弦間での移行**（変ニ音から変ホ音）は、第4指による「変ニ音」から「A線」上におけるハーフ・ポジションへの移行によって始め、同時に「D線」上、第1指による「変ホ音」へと移動する。

17 **隣接する弦間での移行**（変イ音から変ト音）は、第1指による「変イ音」から「G線」上のポジションⅠへのスライドによって始め、同時に「D線」上、第2、第3、第4指による「変ト音」へと移動する。

20頁

18 弓の正しい配分に注意すること。

21頁

19 これらの音の音調は、固有の開放弦を用いて、オクターヴまたはユニゾンで比較せよ。

22頁

20 第3、第4小節目のリズムを演奏する際には、「Z型」のボーイングを用いることができる。すなわち、第4小節目の2分音符を充分な弓で弾くために、第3小節目の第1拍目に対して（軽く）わずかに多めの下げ弓を用い、次に第2、第3拍目の4分音符に対しては、より少なめの弓を用いることを意味する。

23頁

21 弓の割当て：

  a. タイで結ばれた音符の後は 次の4分音符を演奏する準備 のために、**弦上に弓の中央部分を新たに構えなおす**か、もしくは**浮かせて戻す**。

  b. 他の割当と方法は、弓を浮かせて戻すことによらず、タイで結ばれた音符の次に来る最初の上げ弓を、軽やかに、かつ速く用いる。

22 4分休符の間は、弓は弦に触れずに下方で手前に引いておき、その中央部分を「嬰ハ音」の準備として、弦上に置いておく。

例： etc.

23 弓の配分について注意すること。

Page 26.

24 Alternate fingering (refer to Preface—Comment 14):

25 Alternate fingering (refer to Preface—Comment 14):

Page 27.

26 In the fourth position on most basses the thumb touches the base of the neck of the instrument, thereby acting as an aid in locating this position (especially after a rest or silence).

27 Check the intonation of these notes in octaves with the appropriate open string.

Page 28.

28 Remember the same principles of shifting between adjacent strings as explained on page 19.

Page 31.

29 Alternate descending fingering: Shift to the fourth finger on the first note of each measure.

Page 32.

30 Alternate bowing:

etc.

31 Alternate fingering:

  * Student may also begin each two-measure sequence with the fourth finger.

32 Remember that bow compensation is necessary after the dotted quarter note. Refer to page 23 for an explanation.

Page 34.

33 Alternate bowing:

etc.

34 Alternate bowings:

etc.

or

etc.

Page 35.

35 Alternate bowings:

Measures 1 and 2   etc.

Measure 10   etc.

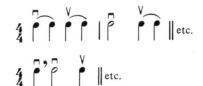

26頁

24 運指法の交替：（序文第14項を参照）：

25 運指法の交替：（序文第14項を参照）：

27頁

26 ほとんどのベースにおいて、親指が楽器のネックの根元に触れるような場合のポジションⅣは、（特に休止符や休みの後で）このポジションを見つけ出すのに助けとなる。

27 これらの音の音調は、オクターヴ関係にある固有の開放弦を用いて確認する。

28頁

28 19頁で説明した、隣接する弦どうしでの移行と同じ原則に注意すること。

31頁

29 下降時の運指法の交替：各小節の最初の音符における第4指への移行。

32頁

30 ボーイングの交替：

etc.

31 運指法の交替：

学習者は、各2小節ごとの反復進行については＊印音を第4指で始めることも可能であろう。

32 付点4分音符の後には、弓の配分の埋合せが必要である。23頁の説明を参照。

34頁

33 ボーイングの交替：

etc.

34 ボーイングの交替：

etc.

または

etc.

35頁

35 ボーイングの交替：

第1、第2小節目：   etc.

第10小節目：   etc.

Page 36.

36 The pressed "G" is possibly used more often when the "G" is preceded by a half or whole step from above or below. When playing a harmonic, touch the "center" of the pitch. Then, if the note or an adjacent note were pressed, it would be in the correct place and in tune.

Page 37.

37 Also practice pressing the "G".

Page 38.

38 Alternate bowings:

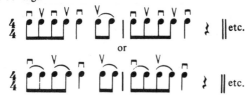

or

39 Alternate bowings:

Page 39.

40 With the advance in technique as well as the wide use of chromesteel strings, notes on all four strings should be learned in this position and throughout the instrument. Refer to the fingering chart at the beginning of the book and learn all the notes in this position and VII Position.

41 Consult the photo chart of Frederick Zimmermann at the beginning of the book for the placement of the left hand in seventh position (which is similar to this position). Many bassists now prefer to place the thumb *on* or *above the string*, a half or whole step below the first finger, in this position and not on the edge of the fingerboard as pictured.

Page 41.

42 Alternate bowings:

Measure 17

Measure 30

Measure 37

Measure 48

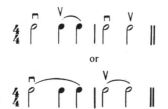

Page 42.

43 Refer to footnotes on page 39. All notes on the D, A and E strings should be learned.

44 Alternate bowings:

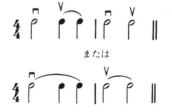

or

36頁

36 おさえて得られる「ト音」は、その「ト音」が上方もしくは下方から、半音または全音で先行されている場合に、より多く使用され得る。
ハーモニックスの演奏をする場合、開放弦の「中央」に触れること。それから、その音もしくは隣接する音がおさえられれば、正しい位置とピッチになるであろう。

37頁

37 この場合も、おさえた「ト音」の練習をすること。

38頁

38 ボーイングの交替：

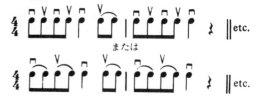

または

39 ボーイングの交替：

39頁

40 クローム・スティール弦の広い利用に加えて、技術の進歩も伴い、このポジションにおける4本の全ての弦上の各音が、学習できるようになった。本書の最初にある運指表を参照し、このポジションと、ポジションⅦの全ての音について学習すること。

41 本書の最初の部分にあるフレデリック・ツィンマーマンの写真による図を参照し、ポジションⅦ（このポジションと同じである）における左手の位置を調べること。今日、多くのベース奏者たちは、親指を写真のように指板のふちに置くのではなく、第1指より半音もしくは全音下方で、**弦上**、もしくは**上方**に置くことをむしろ好む。

41頁

42 ボーイングの交替：

第17小節目：

第30小節目：

第37小節目：

第48小節目：

42頁

43 39頁の脚注を参照。D線、A線、E線の各線上における全ての音が学習されなければならない。

44 ボーイングの交替：

または

Part II.

| | 第II部 |

Page 45.

1 The student is also encouraged to practice the harmonic form of each minor scale throughout this section.

Ex. "A" Harmonic Minor

2 Alternate bowings:

Measure 1

Measure 3

Page 46.

3 Alternate bowing:

4 Alternate bowing:

Page 49.

5 Alternate bowing:

Measure 9

Page 53.

6 Alternate ways to practice thirds:

Page 55.

7 Listen to the four-measure sequence beginning in measure 5.

8 A two-measure sequence predominates this exercise.

Page 56.

9 Four-measure sequence.

10 Maintain a good left-hand position when playing fourths in the early stages of study. Later you may wish to press both strings simultaneously.

45頁

1 学習者は、この章全体を通じて各々の短音階について、和声的短音階の形式でも練習するようにすすめる。

例：イ短調和声的短音階.

2 ボーイングの交替：

第1小節目：

第3小節目：

46頁

3 ボーイングの交替：

4 ボーイングの交替：

49頁

5 ボーイングの交替：

第9小節目：

53頁

6 各3度の練習のための交替方法

55頁

7 第5小節目から始まる4小節ごとの反復進行に耳を傾けること。

8 2小節ごとの反復進行は、この練習曲の特長である。

56頁

9 4小節ごとの反復進行。

10 初期の学習段階における4度の演奏に際しては、左手の位置を正しく保つように。後に、両方の弦を同時におさえるようにすれば良い。

Page 59.

11 Use alternate exercises similar to those suggested for thirds on page 53. In the exercise below press both strings simultaneously and listen carefully to the intonation of the Perfect or Diminished 5th.

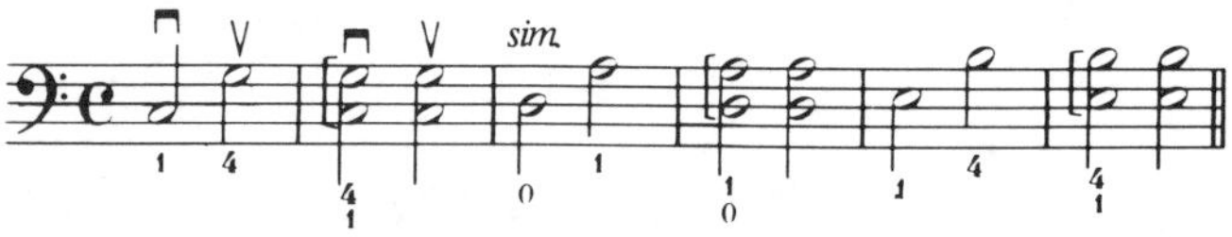

etc.

Page 62.

12 This bowing is recommended, but sixths, sevenths and octaves should also be practiced with the opposite bowing (⊓V).

Page 66.

13 *Preparatory* exercise:

Practice shifting only on the ascending lower note:

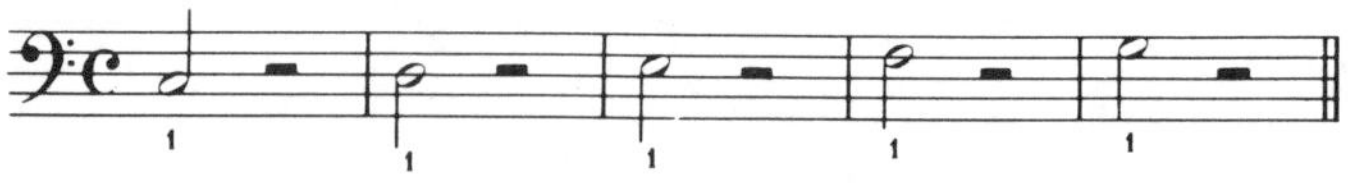

14 *Preparatory* exercise:

Practice shifting only on the descending higher note:

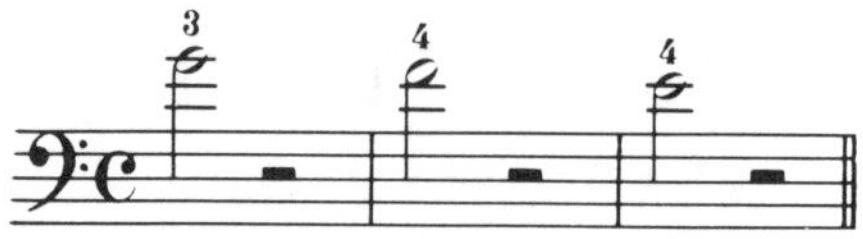

etc.

Part III.

Page 68.

1 Also known as the "portato," "parlando" or "louré" bowing.

Page 69.

2 It is suggested that these bowing articulations be practiced *at first* with the B♭ major scale (ascending and descending) and *then* applied to the above etude. Also, the student should learn the etude *thoroughly*, using separate bows, prior to practicing the bowing variations.

Page 70.

3 Practice these bowing variations in a similar manner as suggested on page 69.

4 This study and exercises on the following pages are examples of "hooked" or "linked" bowing, i.e.

or

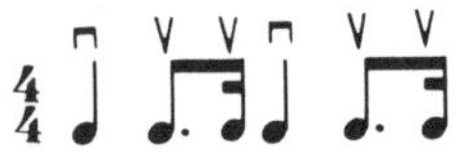

Your teacher should explain *in detail* how to play the bowing articulation for each example. The rhythm may be practiced at first on one pitch or with repeated pitches of a scale. The bowing articulations should be learned before a more difficult left-hand technique is required.

Page 73.

5 Remember to *lift* or *recover* the bow as marked and to proportion the bow correctly according to the rhythmic pattern in exercises 1-15. Set a "realistic" tempo for each exercise.

59頁

11 53頁の3度のところで行った提言と同様の交替練習を用いること。下に示めす練習では、両方の弦を同時におさえ、完全5度または、減5度の音高について注意深く聴くこと。

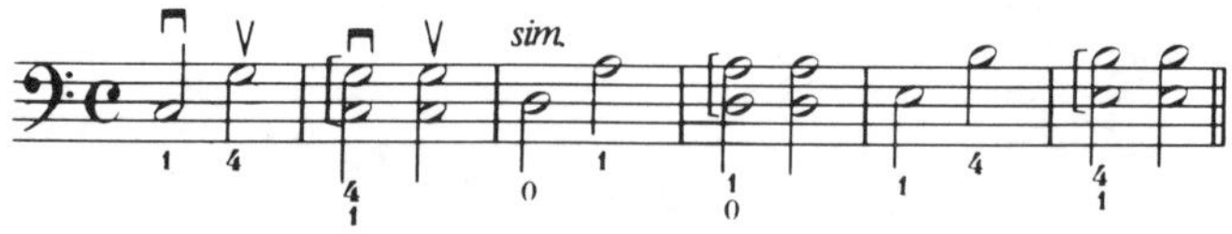

etc.

62頁

12 このボーイングをすすめるが、6度、7度、オクターヴについて、反対のボーイング（⊓V）でも練習すること。

66頁

13 準備練習：

低音の上昇に関する、移行だけの練習：

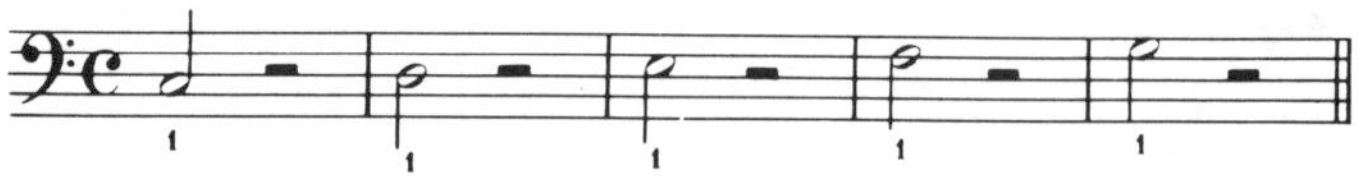

14 準備練習：

高音の下降に関する、移行だけの練習：

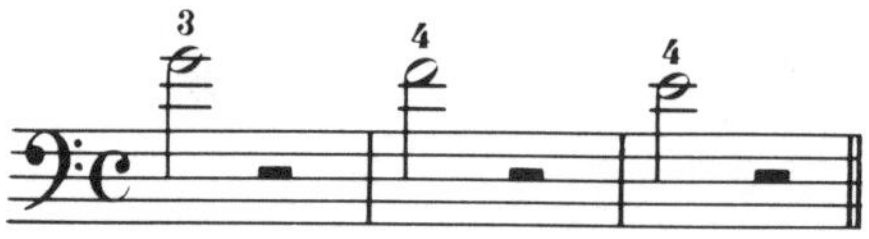

etc.

第III部

68頁

1 「ホルタート」,「ハルランド」,「ルーレ」などの名称でも知られている。

69頁

2 これらのボーイング・アーティキュレーションは、**初め**変ロ長調の音階により（上昇型及び下降型で）練習し、**その後に**上記の練習曲に適用することをすすめる。学習者は、様々なボーイングの練習に入る前に、デタッシェのボーイングによって、この練習曲を**完全に**練習しておかなければならない。

70頁

3 これらの様々なボーイングは、69頁の注と同じ方法により練習すること。

4 続く各頁に現われる練習、及び各練習曲は、「留められた」("hooked")または「連結された」("linked") ボーイングの例である。

（すなわち）

または、

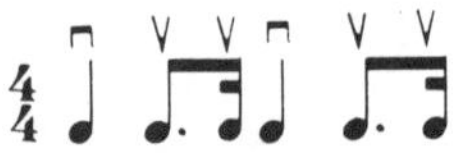

各人の教師は、各々の例に関して、どのようなボーイング・アーティキュレーションで演奏するかということについての**詳細な**説明をしてくれるはずである。リズムは、先ず音階上の1つの音、もしくは、いくつかの音のくりかえしによって練習される。ボーイング・アーティキュレーションは、やらなければならないもっと難しい左手の技術練習に先立って学習されなければならない。

73頁

5 練習曲1～15におけるリズム型に従って、正しい弓の配分と、記されたような弓の**浮かせ戻し**、または**構えなおし**について注意すること。各練習曲については、「現実的な」テンポを設定すること。

Page 76.

6 Hold all quarter notes *full value* and then *lift* or *recover* the bow during the rest.

Page 77.

7 See footnote on page 76.

8 *At all times* the bow must be meticulously balanced and proportioned to avoid false accents.

Page 78.

9 Remember that the descriptions of playing tremolo, pizzicato, etc. throughout the book refer to the "German" bow.

Page 79.

10 Refer to footnote on page 78. Remember pizzicato notes may be played with a variety of lengths and styles similar to bowed passages.

11 Be careful not to set too fast a tempo.

Page 80.

12 German — col legno *geschlagen*

[bow (arco) = bogen]

French — *bois*

13 German — *am Steg*

French — *sur le chevalet*

Page 86.

14 Remember that "slurred staccato" is an *on the string* bowing. Be consistent with the amount and part of the bow used in each exercise.

Page 88.

15 Remember this is an *off the string* bowing (spiccato) and is played in different places (usually between the frog and the middle of the bow) depending on the dynamic. Your teacher should give you specific instructions on tempo, the amount, and part of the bow to be used for exercises 1-5.

Page 89.

16 An alternate fingering would be to have the complete motive in the same position, eliminating the shift.

Part IV.

Page 96.

1 An alternate fingering would be to play the complete mordent in the same position and then shift.

76頁

6 全ての4分音符は、その音価を充分に保たせ、かつ休止符の間では、弓を**浮かせ戻し**、もしくは**構えなおす**こと。

77頁

7 76頁の脚注参照。

8 不正確なアクセントを避けるために、弓は**常に細心の注意をはらって**バランスをとったり、均整をととのえたりしなければならない。

78頁

9 本書全体を通じて、トレモロ、ヒッツィカートなどの演奏に関する記述は、「ドイツ式」弓についてであることに注意すること。

79頁

10 78頁の脚注参照。ヒッツィカートの各音符は、弓で弾かれた各パッセージと同様に、様々な長さと様式で練習されるべきである。

11 テンポを速くしすぎない様に注意する。

80頁

12 独語—コル・レーニョ・**ゲシュラーゲン**（たたく：の意味）
［弓（アルコ）＝ボーゲン］
仏語—ボワ（木：の意味）

13 独——アム・シュテーク（駒の辺で：の意味）
仏語—スール・ル・シュヴァレ（同上）

86頁

14 「スラーの付されたスタッカート」は、**弦上**のボーイングであることに注意すること。各練習曲について使用する弓の量と部分とを首尾一貫させること。

88頁

15 これは**弦を離れる**ボーイング（スピッカート）で、弦の反発力を用いて弓の様々な部分（通常は、毛箱と弓の中央部分の中間で行われるが）で演奏される。各人の教師は、練習曲1～5について使用される特定のテンポ、弓の量と部分などを指示するにちがいない。

89頁

16 運指の交替は、移行をせずに、同一ポジションにおいて正確なリズムをもたらすであろう。

第Ⅳ部

96頁

1 運指の交替は、同一ポジション上で完全なモルデントが演奏でき、それから移行する。

Page 101.

2 Shift smoothly and conserve the amount of bow used when shifting so that the slide will not be accented or exaggerated.

3 Alternate fingerings may be used from this point to the end of the exercise.

Page 102

4 Use very little arm motion when changing strings with the bow. Practice exercises 1-5 softly at first. The amount and part of the bow will be determined in part by the tempo and dynamics used.

Page 104 and 105.

5 The following bowings and articulations may also be practiced:

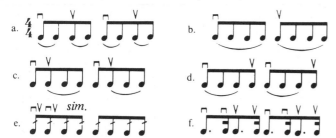

Page 121

6 Originally, measures 1-6 were played by bassists who had instruments with four strings (i.e. low E string) and bassists with instruments with three strings joined in measure 7. Presently, it is performed by the entire bass section throughout. Refer to the Ricordi score for the original articulations of this passage.

7 Alternate bowings (measures 1-3):

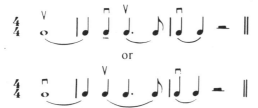

Page 126

8

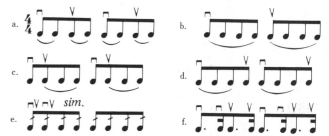

9

Page 127

10

 etc.

Part V.

Page 134.

1 A few alternate bowings and fingerings have been added below the staff.

Page 135

2 In some editions the second eighth note (F♯) is marked *ff*.

3 In some editions there is no ritard.

Lucas Drew

101頁

2 移行はスムーズに、そしてアクセントがついたり、おおげさな移行をしないために、弓の量を一定に保つこと。

3 この位置から、練習曲の終りまで交替運指法による。

102頁

4 弓が他の弦に移る時は、ほんの少しだけ腕の動きを用いる。練習曲1～5は、初めそっと練習する。弓の量と部分は、適用されるテンポと強弱によって決められる。

104～105頁

5 次の各ボーイングとアーティキュレーションでも練習される。

121頁

6 もともと第1～6小節目は、4弦の楽器（すなわち低いE線）を持つベース奏者たちによって演奏され、第7小節目で3弦の楽器を持つたベース奏者たちが加わった。現在は、ベース・セクション全員で演奏される。このパッセージのオリジナル・アーティキュレーションは、リコルディ版のスコアを参照。

7 ボーイングの交替：（第1～3小節目）：

126頁

8

または

9

127頁

10 etc.

第 V 部

134頁

1 いくらかの交替ボーイングと運指は、5線のドに付け加えられている。

135頁

2 いくつかの版では、2番目の8分音符（嬰へ音）は *ff* と記されている。

3 いくつかの版では、*rit.* がない。

ルーカス・ドゥルー

APPENDIX 1:

A facsimile of the Title Page from an earlier Carl Fischer edition of Book I.

付録 1 ：

初期のカール・フィッシャー版第 1 巻の目次のファクシミレ

Neueste Methode

des

Contrabassspiels

von

FRANZ SIMANDL

Mitglied der k. k. Hofkapelle, des k.k. Hofopern Orchesters

und

k. k. Professor am Wiener Conservatorium.

I. THEIL.

Vorbereitung zum Orchesterspiele.

IN LIEFERUNGEN:

1 Lagen
2. Moll=Tonleitern u. Intervalle
3. Strich=u Spiel=Arten etc
4. Verzierungen u Sohreibarten
5. Recitativ- Beispiele

Verfasst
für das Wiener
Conservatorium.

II. THEIL.

Vorbereitung zum Concertspiele
mit Clavierbegleitung.

IN LIEFERUNGEN:

6. Daumeneinsalz u
10 kleinere Etuden
7 9 grosse Etuden
8. Tonleiter- und gebrochene Accord
studien in drei und vierstimmiger
kleiner und grosser Zerlegung
9 Flageolet Arpeggio Doppelgriff.
u 2 Concert Etuden

Verlag & Eigenth.
von
C.F. SCHMIDT, HEILBRONN.

APPENDIX 2:

A facsimile of the Title Page from an earlier German edition listing the sections of Books 1 and 2.

付録 2 ：

初期のドイツ版第 1 及び第 2 巻の目次のファクシミレ

Vorwort.

———

Bei den gegenwärtig großen Anforderungen an das Orchester, im Konzert und im Theater wird, wie bei allen Instrumenten, auch beim Kontrabass eine bedeutende Technik als unbedingt notwendig vorausgesetzt. Es muß sich der Kontrabassist nicht nur bereits eine große Fingerfertigkeit erworben haben, wenn er seine Stelle tüchtig ausfüllen will, sondern er muß auch trachten, sich auf der Höhe der erlangten Technik zu erhalten, um den sich immer mehrenden Aufgaben für sein Instrument Genüge leisten zu können.

Dieses letztere ist nur durch eine fortgesetzte Übung und ein eifriges Selbststudium möglich; der Kontrabassist wird dadurch an Ton gewinnen, seine Kraft und Ausdauer wird sich mehren und seine Fingerfertigkeit kann sich bis zur Virtuosität steigern.

Ja, daß der Kontrabass selbst als Solo- und Konzert-Instrument auftreten kann, dafür liegen gegenwärtig genug Beweise vor.

Ich stellte es mir zur Aufgabe, in diesem Werke eine systematische Anleitung zum Konzertspiele für den Kontrabass zu geben, und will darin den wichtigen und schwierigen Daumeneinsatz, welcher bis jetzt noch primitiv behandelt wurde, reformieren, um dadurch das Solospiel zu erweitern und zu erleichtern. Außer diesen werde ich noch den Schüler mit allen Flageoletten, die zu ungeahnten Effekten verhelfen, bekannt machen und durch progressive Fingerübungen, kleine und größere Etüden die vollständige Vorbereitung zum Konzertspiele bieten.

Wenn meine hier niedergelegten Erfahrungen bei den geschätzten Herren Kollegen eine freundliche Aufnahme finden und den Unterrichtsgang wesentlich erleichtern werden, so fühle ich mich dadurch für die mühevolle Arbeit hinlänglich entschädigt.

Der Verfasser.

Preface.

———

The claims made now-a-days upon both theatre- and concert-orchestras are enormous and naturally also extend to the double-bass, upon which instrument a marvellous technic is expected as an essential condition. Not only must the double-bass-player command great finger-dexterity, if he is to do justice to his art, but he must progress with the times and keep up his technic, having once attained to the required degree of perfection, if he is to master the ever increasing tasks set him.

This it is only possible to do by continual practice and conscientious private study, enabling the double-bass-player to improve his tone, increase his power and strength and render himself a virtuoso on his instrument: for the double-bass is being resorted to more and more as a solo-instrument in our modern concerts.

The object I aim at in publishing the present work, is to afford a systematic method of instruction in double-bass-playing for concert purposes. It is my endeavour to reform the important and difficult thumb-position, — which has hitherto been treated in an exceedingly primitive manner, — with a view to develop and facilitate solo-playing. In addition, I purpose initiating the pupil in all the (artificial) harmonics, enabling him to produce effects, hitherto undreamt of and preparing him in every way for concert-playing, by means of short and long exercises for the fingers.

Should my attempts at improvement based upon personal experience meet with the approval of my colleagues, and facilitate the system of instruction, I shall be amply compensated for the trouble and pains taken in writing this work.

The author.

C. F. S. 2156.

APPENDIX 3:
A facsimile of the Preface to an earlier German edition of Book 2.

付録3：
初期のドイツ版第2巻の表紙のファクシミレ

Cefes Edition.

Neueste Methode	New Method
des	
Contrabass-Spiels	The Double-Bass
von	by

FRANZ SIMANDL

Mitglied der K. K. Hofkapelle, des K. K. Hofopern-Orchesters und Professor am Wiener Konservatorium.	Member of the Imp. Austr. Court Band, Solist and 1st Double-Bassist of the Imp. Court Opera Orchestra and Professor at the Vienna Conservatory.

TEIL I.
Vorbereitung zum Orchesterspiel.
1. Lagen.
2. Moll-Tonleitern und Intervalle.
3. Strich- und Spielarten.
4. Verzierungen und Schreibarten.
5. Recitativ-Beispiele.

PART I.
Initation in Orchestral-playing.
1. The Positions.
2. Minor scales and Intervals.
3. Bowing and manner of playing.
4. Embellishments and Notation.
5. Examples of Recitatives.

TEIL II.
Vorbereitung zum Konzertspiele.
Mit Klavierbegleitung.
6. Daumen-Einsatz und 10 kleinere Etuden mit Pianoforte.
7. 9 grosse Etuden mit Pianoforte.
8. Tonleiter und gebrochene Akkord-Studien.
9. Flageolet, Arpeggio, Doppelgriffe und 2 Konzert-Etuden mit Pianoforte.

Der englische Text wurde revidiert von

Charles Winterbottom
Professor of the Double-Bass at the Royal Academy of Musik, London.

PART II.
Initation in Solo-playing.
With Pianoforte-Accompaniment.
6. Introduction and use of the thumb and ten short studies with Pianoforte-Accompaniment.
7. Nine long studies with Pianoforte-Accompaniment.
8. Studies of scales and arpeggios.
9. Harmonics, Arpeggios, Double-Stopping and 2 Solo-Studies with Pianoforte-Accompaniment.

The text revised by

Charles Winterbottom
Professor of the Double-Bass at the Royal Academy of Music, London.

TEIL III.
Die hohe Schule.
Eine Sammlung hervorragender
Konzert-Etuden, Konzert- und Solostücke
für
Contrabass mit Begleitung des Pianoforte.
Originalbeiträge der bedeutendsten Contrabass-Virtuosen und Lehrer des Contrabass-Spieles.
Band 1, 2, 3, 4, 5, 6, 7, 8, 9.

PART III.
Advanced-Course for the Double-Bass.
Etudes and Concert-Pieces
for the
Double-Bass with Pianoforte-Accompaniment
by eminent Masters and Teachers of the Double-Bass etc.
Vol 1, 2, 3, 4, 5, 6, 7, 8, 9.
Copyright 1903 by C. F. Schmidt.

Verlag und Eigentum von
C. F. SCHMIDT HEILBRONN A. N.

APPENDIX 4:

A facsimile of the Title Page from an earlier German edition listing the complete *Method*.

付録4：

初期のドイツ版総合教則本の目次のファクシミレ

Neueste Methode | Nouvelle Methode | ❋ New Method
des | de | for
Contrabassspieles | Contrebasse | Double Bass
von | par | by

FRANZ SIMANDL.

Theil III.	Partie III.	Part III.

Die hohe Schule. | Cours superieur ❋ ❋ ❋ ❋ de Contrebasse. | Advanced-Course ❋ ❋ for the Double=Bass.

Eine Sammlung hervorragender		
Concert-Etuden, Concert- und Solostücke	Etudes et Pièces de Concert	Etudes and Concert-Pieces
für	pour le	for the
Contrabass mit Begleitung des Pianoforte.	Contrebasse avec accompagnement de Piano	Double-Bass with Pianoforte-Accompaniment
Original-Beiträge der bedeutendsten Contrabass-Virtuosen und Lehrer des Contrabass-Spieles.	par des virtuoses célèbres, professeurs etc.	by eminent Masters and Teachers of the Double-Bass etc.

⎯ INHALT: ⎯

Band 1.
Simandl, Fr. Op. 65. Concert-Etude.
Gregora, Fr. Concert-Etude.
Jakseh, Fr. Elegie.
Lvovsky, B. Drei Stücke nach Corelli.
Schwabe, O. Romanze.
Kukla, C. Impromptu.
Verrimst, V. F. Aire populaire für 3 Contra-
bässe.

Band 2.
Simandl, Fr. Op. 66. Concert-Etude.
Buschmann, L. Albumblatt.
Simandl, Fr. Op. 72. Scherzo capriccioso.
Laska, G. Rhapsodie.
Abert, Jos. Joh. Concert in drei Sätzen.

Band 3.
Simandl, Fr. Op. 70. Concert-Etude.
Kukla, C. Nocturne.
Gregora, Fr. Dumka und Capriccio.
Aubrecht, M. Romanze.
Simandl, Fr. Op. 73. Tarantella.
Hrabe, Jos. Concert.

Band 4.
Simandl, Fr. Op. 71. Concert-Etude.
Chopin, F. Op. 9. Nocturne.
Hegner, L. Andante con variacioni von Haydn.
Haendel, G. F. Concert.
Trautsch, K. Moment de valse.
Moissl, A. Concertstück.

Band 5.
Simandl, Fr. Op 74. Sarabande und Gavotte.
Gianicelli, C. Recitativ und Arie.
Lvovsky, B. Op. 18 Elegie und Burlesca.
Laska, G. Perpetuum mobile.
Simandl, Fr. Op. 75. Concert in 3 Sätzen.

Band 6.
Bearbeitungen von Franz Simandl.
Bach, J. S. Arie und Gavotte.
Domeier, F. „Die Mondnacht", Romanze.
Mozart. Larghetto.
Beethoven. Grosse Arie aus Fidelio.
Mendelssohn. Op. 64. Andante aus dem Violin-
concert.
Beethoven. Op. 50. Romanze.

Band 7.
Simandl, Fr. Op. 35. Notturno.
Simandl, Fr. Op. 32. Phantasie über böhmische
Nationallieder.
Simandl, Fr. Op. 30. Divertissement.
Simandl, Fr. Op. 34. Concertstück.

Band 8.
Simandl, Fr. Op. 76. Cavatine.
Manoly, L. E. Op. 15. Feuille d'Album.
Kleinecke, Rudolf. Fantasie über ungarische
Volkslieder.
Hegner, L. Op. 6. Nocturne.
Symandl, Ad. Op. 20. Sicilienne.
Hegner, L. Op. 5. Legende.
Kukla, L. Fantasie Nr. 2.

Band 9.
Simandl, Fr. Op. 80. Concert-Etude Quasi
Perpetuum mobile.
Moser, L. Romanze und Mazurka.
Danthage, Max. Andante und Humoreske.
Jeissel, Joh. Concertstück.
Misck, Ad. Concert-Polonaise.

Complet in Bänden, sowie in einzelnen Heften zu erhalten, auch werden die Solostimmen einzeln abgegeben.

Band 1, 2, 3, 4, 5, 6, 7, 8, 9
Contrabass mit Pianoforte
Contrabass-Solostimme
Pianoforte-Begleitung

Verlag und Eigenthum
von
C. F. SCHMIDT, HEILBRONN a. N.

APPENDIX 5:

A facsimile of the Title Page from an earlier German edition listing the repertoire of Part III.

付録 5：

初期のドイツ版第III部の目次のファクシミレ

PROGRESSIVE REPERTOIRE

FOR THE DOUBLE BASS – VOL. 1, 2, 3

(with accompanying CD)

It is rare in music pedagogy that something truly revolutionary comes along. *Progressive Repertoire* is the first English language method for beginning Double Bass to incorporate the innovative division of the Bass fingerboard into six positions, developed by renowned French bassist François Rabbath in his three volume *Nouvelle Technique de la Contrebasse*. Mr. Vance has created a method that introduces these revolutionary ideas in a progressive manner using familiar folk and classical material to produce studies and pieces that will appeal to novice bassists of all ages. In addition, a Compact Disc is included with each of the primary books containing all the music performed by François Rabbath, with Elizabeth Azcona-Hartmark, piano.

Progressive Repertoire for Double Bass will introduce American teachers and students to the most important new techniques developed for the instrument in the last 100 years.

Progressive Repertoire for the Double Bass – George Vance:

O5427 – Volume 1 (with Annette Costanzi) – (ISBN 0-8258-3329-9)
O5426 – Volume 1 – Piano Accompaniment – (ISBN 0-8258-3328-0)
O5428 – Volume 2 – (ISBN 0-8258-3330-2)
O5462 – Volume 2 – Piano Accompaniment – (ISBN 0-8258-3927-0)
O5429 – Volume 3 – (ISBN 0-8258-3331-0)
O5463 – Volume 3 – Piano Accompaniment – (ISBN 0-8258-3928-9)

Also by George Vance,

VADE MECUM

A wonderful compendium of scales, arpeggios and bowing variations, *Vade Mecum*, is a manual that will greatly help to enhance the technical dexterity of string bass players. It is a terrific resource of materials for daily practice and pre-performance warm-up exercises.

O5425 – Vade Mecum – George Vance – (ISBN 0-8258-3327-2)

FROM THE FOREWORD:

I am happy to present to you the George Vance method, *Progressive Repertoire for the Double Bass*. Often, the lack of musicality discourages people who use traditional methods. George Vance's method, on the other hand, consists entirely of well-known tunes with clear fingering especially suited to beginners. Everyone, no matter what performing level, will find real pleasure in playing these melodies.

— François Rabbath

COMMENTS BY PROFESSIONALS:

George Vance has produced a new approach to the teaching of double bass which has resulted in an excellent method for both the young and the adult beginner and the advanced player. His design of introducing primarily the intervals of octaves, fifths and fourths is a logical step to ready the student for the smaller intervals which are not as easy to hear accurately. His system is a superb preparation for the aspiring student to pursue other methods of higher technique, such as that of François Rabbath. Having worked with Vance's unique method and ideas, and observing his plan in action, I enthusiastically endorse his books.

— Anthony Bianco
Principal Bass Laureate,
Pittsburgh Symphony Orchestra

Great results from your method have manifested yet again, in brilliant playing during a master class at the Curtis Institute from a player I started at age 9. Thanks for your dedication.

— Paul V. Ellison
Professor of Double Bass, Rice University
President, International Society of Bassists